The Education *of a* TEACHER

Lessons a Small Town Taught a Teacher

NOEL NATION

SCRIPTOR HOUSE
THE EPITOME OF GREATNESS

Scriptor House LLC

2810 N Church St Wilmington, Delaware, 19802

www.scriptorhouse.com

Phone: +1302-205-2043

Published by Scriptor House LLC

Paperback ISBN: 979-8-88692-274-5

eBook ISBN: 979-8-88692-275-2

Hardback ISBN: 979-8-88692-276-9

The Education *of a* TEACHER

Lessons a Small Town Taught a Teacher

NOEL NATION

THE EDUCATION OF A TEACHER
LESSONS A SMALL TOWN TAUGHT A TEACHER

"When you're dealing with people,

You do a whole lot better if

you go not so much by the book,

But by the heart." — Barney Fife on

The Andy Griffith Show

Episode#61

EDUCATION: A REFLECTION

"You're a mother f'n 'd'!" is what I heard come out of a 6th-grade special education student's mouth after telling him to quit kicking another kid while waiting on the bus to leave school. While trying to keep my composure, I responded, "Come here!" I gave him another chance, thinking maybe I just heard him wrong. "What did you say!?" Being a short kid, he walked up to me, put his chin on the bottom of my chest, and looked up at me. He slowed down and said, "He made me mad, *yefferdy*!" I looked down at him, and instead of pounding him like a hammer on a nail, I refrained from laughing as I stated, "You still can't kick him!" This was a scenario I had never had in mind while going to college. I rolled back in my memory banks to see how in the world I ended up here. I have been in education for thirty-plus years. Have I done what I set out to do? Is this what I wanted to accomplish in my life?

In the following days, I reflected on the thirty years to the time I was driving to Cleveland for the first time. "Do I want to do this?" This is the question I asked myself as I was driving out to my final interview in Cleveland, OK. I grew up 40 miles away, in Tulsa, and never even knew this place existed. Do I want to be a teacher? Much less do I want to teach in the "sticks?" I grew up at a local recreation center in the city with wide open spaces to run and jump. This town has a dike surrounding it to keep the nearby lake from flooding it. Have the people here ever been on the other side of the dike? Do they know how the rest of civilization lives? Do they even know there is civilization "on the other side"? There would be a need to adjust to the new life I had been talked into taking.

Teaching was not my original intent when I began college. I wanted to be a doctor, but my desire to play baseball and a lack of desire to study warranted a change in my major. That need came to a head when my immunology professor had to tutor me one too many times, and in her Lebanese accent, said, "Get out! You no good!" She simply meant, in translation, "Please change your major!

I'm tired of tutoring you while your brain is somewhere else!" So, after speaking with many friends and acquaintances, who said I explained things to them very well and thoroughly, I changed it to Physical Education with a Minor in Science, which led to me taking science education and coaching classes. I was headed down the road that led me to teach. I performed much better in that capacity if I do say so myself.

It's not something I set out to do for the rest of my professional life, but I launched that part of my career. Little did I know, all the things I learned before I became a teacher that prepared me to be an effective teacher. Little did I know of all the things I would learn as a teacher over the next 30-plus years. Little did I know what kind of response I would have if someone ever called me a "mother f'n 'd'."

THE FOUNDATION OF EDUCATION: FAMILY

One of my favorite publications is "Poor Richard", otherwise known as, "Poor Richard's Almanack" written by Benjamin Franklin. From that come many well-known sayings, such as: "An ounce of prevention is worth a pound of cure" and "Well done is better than well said." Another, not so popular but true, saying is "Observe all men, thyself most." I have incorporated many of these sayings of "wisdom" in my life, especially that of observing. Many things in my life have caused me to look inward before I make a move on anything. To get where I was bound to go, I had to start somewhere.

I was born the third of three boys. My dad, Clarence, was a World War II veteran who had a tremendous work ethic and taught me that *I can try and fail, and try and fail, and try and fail again. But I won't be a failure unless I fail to try again.* That was a simple but life-making statement that I have kept close by in all situations. My mom, Mary, was a classy lady who was raised on a farm in central Oklahoma and was admired by the countless people she came into contact within the business world. Both of my parents made sure my family was well grounded in the faith. My oldest brother asked if we were going to church. Dad responded quickly, "Is it Sunday?"

My brothers were 10 and 6 years older than me. The oldest, Larry, had interests in life that included sports and making money. He wanted Mom and Dad to name me Lefty, after his favorite baseball player, Lefty Gomez. My other brother, Garry, was very musical and studied a lot. Growing up, I had to sit between them everywhere we went. I was the buffer.

I was told that my name was going to be "Barry." I am very thankful it was not. When Mom or Dad called for Larry or Garry, they both answered. So, they had to come up with an alternative. Noel was it. Born in the middle of the summer, I received a unique name that fires up every year around Christmas time. Early on, I took on two characteristics that have held true throughout my life. I have been an observer. Both of my brothers let it be known that I was to be seen and not heard. . That relegated me to watching things and people and soaking in everything around me. I also felt a need to be accepted, and part of that was the desire to be useful. I wanted to do things that would give people a reason to like me. I developed a tremendous desire to meet the approval of the people who meant the most to me.

My first real opportunity to feel accepted and needed came toward the end of my 8th-grade year when the morning newspaper route in my neighborhood became available. I inquired about it and was given a chance. On my first day, I woke up at 3:30 a.m. and traveled ½ mile on a bicycle to my pick-up point where my route manager met me and began my one-night training. We put my bicycle in his truck along with the papers, and away we went back to my neighborhood. He folded the papers and shined a light on the houses I was to throw the papers at. The time was 4 a.m. on the first of February. It was cold, but pleasant. What great fun! What a great experience! I had my first job, I was ready for more, and I felt useful!

On February 2nd, I was by myself. My route manager gave me a list of houses, and I was set to succeed. Bedtime was early, but 3:30 am came early. I got dressed and went outside to find the temperature 20 degrees colder than the previous night, windy, and spitting sleet. What a shock to my system! However, I was on my own. I was going to do it! The weather for the rest of the week was not any better. It seemed worse. Each night, 3:30 am came earlier and earlier. The ride up to my paper drop got longer and longer. I hated it! I went to my mother and expressed my disdain for this paper route, even though it was a stupid idea for even wanting a job to begin with. After all, I was just a kid. I had my whole life to have a job. I wanted to quit.

Mom, in all her wisdom, told me I wouldn't get paid for the work I had already done if I quit right now. She talked me into working at least until the end of the month to get paid, and also, in the meantime, we might work together to come up with a plan to make it easier. The suggestion seemed reasonable. I was up to that task. Work a month, get paid, and then go about being a kid again.

She and my dad helped me get organized. We developed a map and a plan. I worked on the plan and made it to the end of the month. Despite my desire to work for only a month, much to my surprise and much to my dismay, I started to enjoy it. I liked it even more when I went around to collect money and realized that I had money. On top of that was the prestige of being an 8th grader and having a steady job. Most of the kids I went to school with were still being "supported" by their parents, their very wealthy parents. I had the amazing satisfaction of earning the money I had.

What I learned from that whole situation has stuck with me my entire life. It was the fact that if I had quit when I wanted to, when it got hard, without trying to get organized and working at it, I would have quit everything else when it got difficult. Believe me. Later in my life, there would be plenty of opportunities to quit, both athletic and career. My oldest brother's constant reminder, "When the going gets tough, the tough get going," came into play here. He would also, in an attempt to keep me from going to mom after making me cry, tell me to "be a man!" I remembered these words, too. All this advice was sandwiched around, "When I want your opinion, I'll beat it out of you."

Until then, the only thing I had done that was tough was playing football. My knees and my heels hurt terribly at the end of each practice. I couldn't stand it, so I quit. I had never felt like that before. I later found out that my knees hurt because of Osgood-Schlatter disease, which would be with me the rest of my life, and I would have to endure a certain amount of pain each time I was physically active, and my heels were suffering from a condition that, to this day, I don't know what was wrong other than that the nurse gasped when she saw my X-ray and the doctor said, "No more sports, ever!" It killed me inside.

After two years of no baseball, no basketball, and no football, my heels got better, and I received a medical clearance. I began to play baseball again, but I regret never going back to playing football. Getting to coach football while teaching at the high school level was reward enough. I still held on to what I learned as an 8th grader. I will not quit something I start because it may be too tough. I will do my best to see it through.

Another learning experience I had that helped me in my professional life was when I got cut from my high school baseball team. My coach told me he "didn't have a place" for me. I thought he was crazy. He was not an excellent coach if he couldn't see my talents. The guys who played in front of me weren't that good. They certainly weren't better than me! At least, that's what I thought. I came up with a whole lot of excuses; however, I was determined to prove my coach wrong and set out to find a place to walk on and play college baseball. After all, I wasn't finished playing baseball. I had a goal of playing professional ball, and I just couldn't end my career by being cut in high school!

I held those thoughts of blaming my high school coach until I got to Northeastern Oklahoma A&M College in Miami, OK and saw the other athletes. My brain exploded with the thought, "Holy cow!" Were my eyes opened?! I realized how far behind physically I was from everyone else. I wasn't near as good as I thought I was. (This was an attitude I would also have to deal with as a teacher/coach in the future.) I desperately had to make up time. Kicking in my idea of not quitting, I started a workout regimen on my own and got ready for tryouts. I got myself physically ready, or at least more so than I would have been otherwise.

On the first day of tryouts, over 80 guys came. I looked around and thought that my work was cut out for me. I was up to the challenge. The training I did gave me much more confidence. The coach told us to throw our gloves over to the sidelines and start running. Along with the 80 other guys, I did. After the first lap, we all stopped and started to pick up our gloves. The coach told us to put the gloves away and keep running. We ran all the practice. We did not pick up a ball. The coach dismissed the team with instructions to practice the next day. Comments from the 80 guys included, "I came here to play baseball, not run track!" That was the nicest thing I heard.

The next day, I was one of 40 guys that showed up. We did the same thing. Fortunately for me, I didn't know any better. I thought this was the way things were done in college baseball. It had nothing to do with my desire not to quit. That was the first thing that helped me understand the many things I was naïve about. The coach ended practice with instructions for practice tomorrow, and the grumblings of most of the guys continued.

The next day, I was one of 30 guys to show up. Hallelujah! After he stopped us and told us to grab our gloves and a partner to play catch. Cheers rang up to the heavens, and I was able to take the next step in my quest for pro baseball. I learned that a desire to succeed, along with patience, equates to perseverance, which will help anyone achieve a goal. Not to mention, I have no clue how some things are done.

I finally got my chance to play at Northeastern Oklahoma A&M College with a minimal amount of success, but enough success to open the door to walk on, again, this time at the Southwest Baptist University in Bolivar, MO. Here is where I had a third experience that took me to where I was going, pointing me toward an eventual teaching career. Once I arrived at Southwest Baptist, I did not struggle as a pitcher, but I still had not gained the full confidence of my coach. I had a great work ethic, so my coach said, which was aided by the teammates I was closest to having the same ideals.

Southwest Baptist was a small, private NAIA school, and my coach doubled as the women's basketball coach. We were to play the number two team in NCAA Div. 2, Southwest Missouri . State University, now known as Missouri State. On the same day, a 6'4" girl was making her visit to our campus. The coach planned to give the team to the assistant coach, make me the starting pitcher, and show the recruit around the campus and town. He would come as soon as he could after the game started, and, hopefully, it wouldn't be too far out of hand when he got there, so he could make the necessary adjustments.

We started the game, and the coach, Duane Trogdon, brought his recruit to the field to see how the game was progressing. He soon left to continue showing her around, and we carried on without him. When he got back and found out that we were ahead, I saw his jaw drop. He couldn't believe it. I had shut down a highly potent offense, and we had scored four runs against one of the best pitchers in Division 2. We ended up winning 4-3. My spot in the coach's heart became big, and my spot as the "go-to guy" was solidified. My life lesson learned was that hard work does pay off.

I went on to have a very solid career and, at one time, was even scouted by three pro teams and was the team MVP in 1981. I did not achieve pro status, as was my dream, but I can rest assured that I put forth my best effort and did not quit when it would have been easier to do so. These are just a few experiences that helped with grooming during my pre-teaching career. I have, many times, reflected on them and used what I learned in teaching and coaching others.

I believe the greatest motivation source a school-aged child has is the family. The early years of development are almost solely in the family. Attitudes about life, relationships, and even future endeavors are formed at this time, all this before attending one day of school. My dad had always been supportive of what I tried to accomplish. Much of the time I was growing up and competing, he was unable to attend because he was working out on the road. I always wanted to please Dad. I always knew I did, but he never "said" so. I received confirmation one day after I had been a teacher for nearly 20 years. He constantly worked on puzzles, whether they were crosswords or cryptoquips. In the mail came a package from him. I opened it to find that he had solved a cryptoquip and framed it. It was a quote from Los Angeles Dodgers manager Tommy Lasorda. It read, "The difference between the impossible and the possible lies in a man's determination." At the bottom of the quote, he wrote, "a description of Noel." I always knew it, but now it is confirmed. It would have been nice to have coached and taught kids with a backing like that at home.

PHASE 2: EDUCATION'S NEXT STEP

As stated earlier, I have always been an observer. Sometimes, as an active participant, I feel as if my observing certain things kept me from participating. That is not always a bad thing—not participating.

Early in my collegiate career, I met a fellow named Steve brown. He had a desire to be called "Maddog". He constantly did things to try to live up to the nickname. One incident came during a weekend when few people stayed in the dorm. Northeastern A&M College in Miami, OK. It was known as a bedroom college. Most people who stayed during the week in a dorm would go home on the weekend for various reasons. Those who stayed were usually international students or those few who lived too far away to travel home often. While in the 1st-floor lounge on a Saturday evening, those of us left in the dorm—about a dozen and a half—were watching reruns of Bonanza and Star Trek when we heard a yell at the end of the hallway. It sounded something like a "Tarzan" yell. At that time, we heard a "thumping splat." We hurried to the door, going down the hall to see a sprawled-out body of "Maddog" at the bottom of the far stairs in a puddle of blood. The dorm proctor called the ambulance while the rest of us ran down to see what happened. It turns out that "Maddog", once again trying to prove his nickname, tied a garden hose to the top railing, three stories up, and swung down in a Tarzan fashion. Little did he realize, until it was too late, that the hose would snap under his weight and render him helplessly free fall to the bottom of the staircase. We found him in very poor condition, to say the least.

Steve survived the fall, but I learned a very important lesson in the whole situation. I learned that **I don't have to experience something to know I ought not to do it!** I have applied this to many situations in my life that, I believe, have kept me out of trouble and healthy.

Furthermore, I formed an idea about alcohol while observing Steve and many others in my life, and have chosen not to drink alcoholic beverages. It was a simple choice, and I lived my life accordingly. I have been ridiculed, made fun of, and called names because of that choice, but my only response is that of letting people know why I have made my choice. The reasons came from the likes of those who have ridiculed me. I have narrowed my reasoning down to four incidents, although there are many more to choose from.

My first real experience with alcohol came at Edison Junior High School in Tulsa, OK. I was in gym class in 9th grade.

All participants were to wear white shirts, white shorts, and white socks, all with our names stenciled in black on them. I think it was so the teacher could call us by name without having to know our names. All the guys were getting dressed in the locker room when a murmur went through the rows of lockers of "Chaz" being drunk. Somewhere between the second and third hours, Chaz got wasted. One of the guys said, "Follow me. Do what I do." So, all the guys went into the gym and started mulling around, waiting for the coach to start class and for "Chaz" to enter. He did. He was staggeringly drunk. I was amazed. I had, up to this point in my life, never seen a drunk person. The leader in the locker room began, "It's too bad about Chaz. We sure are going to miss him." Another chimed in, "Yeah, it's too bad he had to die." This got the attention of Chaz—at least the attention he could give. He tried to respond by saying, "I'm not dead, guys. See? I'm right here!" The others continued to pretend Chaz was dead. Despite his efforts, Chaz was not as convincing as the guys in the class. He even tried to get physical. He was getting mad. There was quite a commotion, and it was getting loud with laughter, and the class of about 75 9th-grade boys had encircled the helplessly plastered Chaz. He passed out about the time the gym teacher put his paper down to see what all the noise was about. I never threw any insults out at Chaz and did not pretend, like most of the others, but I admit, I laughed, uncontrollably. There were 74 boys that day who had a good time. One did not. I dare say, though, that he didn't remember it. I learned something important that day. **When you are drunk, people make fun of you.** I did not want to be in the position that Chaz had put himself into. Another incident that helped me decide to not drink alcohol also came at Northeastern

A&M. It involved a guy I had grown up with. His name was Brett. He was a super-talented pitcher for the baseball team. I had played against Brett in Little League and played on the same team in high school. That is until I got cut from my high school team. I was too naïve to think that my playing days were over, so I found a place that would allow me to walk on. That turned out to be Northeastern A&M, the same place Brett received a scholarship to play.

It was the beginning of my second year at NEO. I had made it through the first year as a walk-on, and the coach invited me back to be a non-scholarship player. Once again, I was too naïve to quit. He told me that he liked my work ethic and that he might have a chance to make the lineup soon. I was excited.

Brett was scheduled to start a Saturday game. The night before, he and a few of his buddies "went up north." They crossed the state line into Kansas so they could drink legally. The legal drinking age in Oklahoma was 21, and in Kansas, it was 18. Brett got drunk, and his buddies left him there.

The next morning, as the team gathered before the game, the coach was giving final instructions and handing out newly laundered uniforms. He came to Brett's number and hollered for him. No answer. He hollered again. Still, no answer. A little perturbed, the coach looked at me and said, "Well, nation, you have earned your uniform. I have just the one to give you." It was Brett's. I was ecstatic. I didn't necessarily want Brett's uniform, but, as the saying goes, "it worked for me!" I suited out and even got to pitch that day. Furthermore, I threw 3 shutout innings and suited out every game after that. It was no longer Brett's uniform. It was mine. He sobered up and had to get a different one. I got a chance and ran with it. Through that situation, I was able to receive a scholarship offer from Southwest Baptist University and was named MVP for the 1981 season. I learned another valuable lesson about alcohol. When you are drunk, you lose opportunities to those who are not drunk.

A situation that truly solidified my thoughts about alcohol also came at NEO. After a football game on a Saturday night, my roommate, RJ, and I returned to our dorm room like every other post-game ritual. The room was what I refer to as the "arm-pit" of rooms. It was across the hall from the community restroom. It smelled. It was noisy. It was not the best place to be after a baseball game. We did what we always did. We tried to get "holed" up in our room to avoid any extracurricular activity that may occur near the restroom area.

The noise grew a little louder than normal, and the commotion lasted a little longer than normal. We opened the door to find out why. Directly in front of our door lay a fellow who had passed out drunk. If RJ and I had wanted to leave the room, we would have had to step over him. Several guys on the dorm wing were standing around staring at him. He began to heave and then throw up. Everyone stepped back a bit and then looked at RJ and me as if to say, "What are you going to do about this?"

We started a little longer when I sent someone to get the dorm proctor. We stared some more as we waited. The proctor finally got there, put his hands on his hips, and thought a moment. He then reached down, grabbed the ankles of the drunken fellow, and began to drag him down the hall. We followed. The proctor found an unoccupied room, opened the door, slid the drunken body into it, slapped his hands together as if to wipe them clean, and said, "He can sleep it off in here." Everyone that followed went back to their rooms except me. I just stood there and thought about what I had witnessed. Another situation that helped me choose alcohol. **When you are drunk, you lose your worth as a person.**

For many years, I held on to these experiences as my reasons for not imbibing alcoholic beverages. Then another one came across my desk that put an exclamation point on my belief: On March 29, 2010, MSNBC.com reported that a Pennsylvania man, approximately 65 miles northeast of Pittsburgh along Route 36 in Oliver Township, had been charged with public drunkenness after he was seen trying to resuscitate a dead possum. A witness reported seeing him attempt to give mouth-to-mouth resuscitation to the roadkill. The man's name was widely circulated on the internet, causing significant humiliation for him and his family. This incident highlights that, when intoxicated, individuals may face considerable embarrassment, impacting both themselves and their families.

These examples and plenty more helped me choose to never take part in drinking alcoholic beverages. These situations helped educate me in certain areas of my life, and also aided the way I treated people. It's ironic how the decisions a person makes in life affect their outcome.

THE EDUCATIONAL MENAGERIE: COLLEGE

Going away to school thrust me into a whole new way of learning. I now had to learn things, both intentional and unintentional, from people who did not grow up in my backyard or nearby. The things I came away with from the dorms and campus were things I was able to use on the job as a teacher, coach, and administrator.

I went "potluck" as far as roommates were concerned, and that concerned me. Who was I going to be placed with? What kind of guy would he be? Would he and I have a lot in common and be good friends, or would he say, "Mind your own business?" Whoever he was—he never showed up. Several others who signed up also never showed up. So we were left with the task of finding a roommate, so there wouldn't be three guys in a room. RJ and I ended up as roommates. He was from Oswego, KS. Great first impression; we hit it off just fine. He, too, was from a good, strong family and had a decent high school athletic career. One thing I don't think I ever got used to was that he put the red and blue ribbons he won while showing hogs at county and state fair competitions up on our wall. In the shape of his initials. He was proud of his accomplishments, real proud. I made fun of him for it. I think I was relentless in doing so. It comes down to the fact that he had accomplished something, and I felt I had not. I also made comments about his questions. He asked things that he already knew the answer to. One day, several of the guys were in our room just talking, and Roy said, "Well, I guess I better go do my physics homework." RJ looks at him and said, "You have physics?" "No, I just have the homework!" Thus, it was the birth of the "RJ question." I had a lot of fun. I don't think he did. It took me a while to understand where other people come from and the fact that they have feelings. I was relentless with my "cut-downs" and did not take into consideration that, in my trying to be funny, someone else was getting hurt emotionally and socially.

I think I grew up before we parted ways from college. Years later, he gave me a call. Our children, near the same age, were participating in athletics in rival schools. We got together for dinner and, to this day, are dear friends.

Another roommate, Mike, was planning on becoming a preacher. He came from a wonderful, tight-knit family from Commerce, OK. He was the one who introduced me to Southwest Baptist University, and we traveled there together. We had great times, with tremendous memories. However, as I learned ever so slowly, when you live with or are around someone so much, you may have difficult times. One incident came when, after a weekend trip home, Mike brought back some scrumptious cookies from home. He shared them with me, and I was truly grateful. A few nights later, Mike was out visiting his girlfriend, and I, not having a girlfriend at the time, was asked to go down the hall and play cards. Great! I'll bring some snacks. I picked up the cookies and headed down. We had a great time. That is until Mike came home and wanted a cookie. He came to ask me about them, only to see the serving tray full of crumbs. They were all gone. He threw a minor fit. At which time I did what I do best and made fun of him for it. I never once thought about him. It was me. Weeks later, he went home again. He brought cookies back to school. This time, he walked to where we were playing cards, had a cookie in his hand, and proudly proclaimed, "I have the best cookies in the world! You know! You've had them. But, today and forever, you will not be partaking again!" Then he left. We laughed. I thought of making a humorous retort but stopped myself. I was the one at fault. He was just letting me know, for once, that I was wrong in my actions. I learned that what someone shares with me is not mine to share with others. It's only sharing if it's mine!

Thousands of stories came out of college. Roy taught me about how hard work pays off. He was 24 years old when he started school and wanted to play baseball as well. He would go to practice, go to supper, do his homework, and go outside and swing at a piece of paper on a "t" with a bat for an hour or more, then go to the shower and bed. We would talk about hitting and pitching for hours at a time. He helped make me a better pitcher. As the Bible says in Proverbs 27:17, "iron sharpens iron."

Steve was the fellow I met on the first day of school who considered himself a health nut and wanted to be called "Maddog." He constantly did things that would, to him at least, warrant being called just that. Several mornings, we were awakened by what sounded like a shotgun blast. Steve confided in me that it was him, and he was shooting at the library. "Why." "Because I want to." He rolled a bowling ball down the hallway, back and forth, often. He was also the one who played the role of Tarzan in the dorm. While visiting students for the Baptist student union one day, another fellow, who was about three to four inches taller than me, knocked on Steve's door. He answered the door with a shotgun pointed right at me. The fellow with me dove down behind me as best he could. I took my index finger and put it on the barrel of

The shotgun slid to the side, pointing it away from me, and I proceeded to tell Steve why we had come to his room. Although Steve didn't allow too many people to be friends with him, I realized I was one for a reason. He started coming to the BSU from time to time after that. I haven't seen him since graduation, but I hope his life has less turmoil. I learned how to deal with attitudes about life other than mine.

All the book knowledge I was gaining while in college classes was a good thing. The lessons I learned from dealing with RJ, Mike, Roy, and Steve, as well as countless other people and situations, proved to be priceless. I had to deal with the countless people I had no idea I was about to meet in a place I had never known existed.

PURE EDUCATION:
LIFE, LOVE, AND TRAGEDY

Coming into a teaching job single didn't seem like a daunting task to me. It may have been better that I started my career single because I used my time at home alone to study for my next day's lesson. This was hard for me in school because there were so many people around to not study with.

After a few years of dating off and on, I fell in love with a hometown girl. I didn't realize until years after I came to Cleveland that she was with a lady who was showing me a rental house before I even moved there. We did not start dating until after she graduated, but that did not keep the locals from talking. My principal at the time came into my classroom, shut the door behind him, turned a chair backward, sat down, and asked, "Be truthful with me. Are you dating Amy Spess?" I looked at him, leaned forward, and said, "No. But I'm going to go as soon as school is out." "That's good enough for me", he responded as he left the room. That was the last I heard from him, or too many others on the subject.

We were married a year and a half later and started a family a year and a half after that. I was coaching high school girls basketball at the time and was involved in a tournament in Bristow around the due date of our firstborn. Schools all around the state had been canceled for snow and ice for two days. The tournament was canceled as well. My wife woke me early Friday, January 8, and said, "It's time!" After getting ready, we went to her parents' house to pick up her mother and headed to the hospital. It was 5 degrees and icy that morning. No one in their right mind would have gotten on that road. That was the first realization that I had about children. They don't have the right mind when it's time to be born.

We got on the road to Tulsa fairly easily to find that there were a lot of people who were not in their right mind. They had to be at work in Tulsa. They wanted to drive in the not-so-icy lane, and they did not want to drive fast. It was icy, really icy. Amy, my wife, was writhing in labor pains as I felt I needed to hurry, so I shifted my GMC Jimmy into a 4-wheel drive and "eased" onto the middle lane of the highway, which had not been snow plowed. I began to pass car after car on the way to the hospital. We received many stares, frightened and angry stares, but I was going to get to the hospital before the baby was born. There was one more problem: my heater thermostat was stuck and did not allow the heater to warm up the vehicle. While passing cars, speeding in the icy lane, with a pregnant lady shifting back and forth in the passenger seat, I was scraping ice off the inside of the windshield to see. All this, with a lady in the back seat just sitting, shivering under a blanket.

We made it, by the grace of God, to the hospital, and I helped my wife out and to the door of the hospital. I then ran back to help my mother-in-law out of the car so she could go to the driver's seat and park it. I ran back to the hospital entrance to find my wife seated on the floor because she could walk no further. "Hold on! Hold on!" There were supposed to be wheelchairs here! I ran to the other side of the lobby to retrieve one and ran back. I could feel the clock ticking and my soon-to-be daughter was holding the watch. I ran with my wife in the wheelchair, to the elevators and got her to the maternity ward for delivery. It was too late for an epidural, but it was not too late for me to wash up and witness the birth of my first child, a beautiful girl named Anna Elizabeth.

I coached girls' basketball for another year. I then became the athletic director for the high school, while retaining my football and baseball coaching duties. Annabeth was very visible throughout the school and community. She "cut her teeth" on the basketball court and football field. A lady in town made her a tiger uniform, and she would be with the cheerleaders while they performed during games. After a football game, the thrill of winning did not compare to seeing her run across the field to congratulate me with a huge hug. She was the darling around the athletes and cheerleaders and, even more so, for the family. She was three years old when she was a flower girl for a springtime coronation. Annabeth was a beautiful child who made us very proud.

On May 20, 1991, my wife was three days overdue with our second child. The whole school seemed to be waiting for me to "get the call". The night before, I had helped as a senior sponsor, with the baccalaureate services, and the students were anxiously awaiting the end of the school year. A call came over the school intercom that I was to come to the office for a phone call. The students knew that it may just be what I was waiting for, time to go to the hospital. As I walked through the lunchroom, kids were patting me on the back, and giving me high-fives in their anticipation of the blessed event, saying, "Way to go, 'Dad! Go get 'em." It was a very proud moment for me. Upon getting to the office, I found quite a different set of news. My wife, while on the way to Tulsa, with her mother, grandmother, aunt, and Annabeth, were hit by a drunk driver. My father-in-law, Amy's sister, her husband, and I sped to Tulsa to find out that the only survivor in the accident was Amy. She had suffered many injuries to the point of me not recognizing her while she lay in the emergency room before life-saving surgery.

Years ago, I made the decision not to partake in alcohol based on what I had seen it do to the people I was near. Yet, even though my family had nothing to do with alcohol, it now has torn us apart. The choice someone else made to drink affected my whole family. Along with my wife's mother, grandmother, and aunt, the deaths of my two daughters had a tremendous effect on the school. What they would call a "dangerous decision" took the life of a young child whom the entire student body saw a significant amount of life from. Over the coming months, the community, school, and students received an enormous amount of love and support. The students seem to reflect in their own lives about their decisions and the resolutions they would make in the future.

I learned that the identity of a community, especially a small town, comes through the school. How the school goes is how the community goes. People get together in the coffee shops and restaurants and talk about the school, whether it is sports or personalities. They see each other at the grocery store or hardware store, whether it is good or bad. They talk about school matters. What a drunk driver did to my family truly affected an entire community.

My wife recovered from a six-week-long coma and is still confined to a wheelchair, which is a constant reminder of that tragic day. The school continues to show love and support. Even though the students are different year in and year out, they have followed the pattern set by those students who were first-hand witnesses of the outpouring of affection and continue to do so.

ADJUSTMENT IN EDUCATION: GAME CHANGERS

During the course of my "Educating The Future Educator" classes at Southwest Baptist University, I had the opportunity to watch a short film entitled, "Cipher In The Snow", distributed by Brigham Young University in 1973. It told of a young man, Cliff Evans, who walked off a bus on the way to school and fell over, dead, in the snow. The rest of the film had his "favorite" teacher, a man who said he had little contact with the boy, trying to find out what caused this to happen. The teacher looked at Cliff's school records and talked with his "family" to find clues. He concluded that the boy was just "erased" from his surroundings. He became a "nothing", a "zero", a "cipher". He died for lack of anyone he cared about, caring about him. It made an immediate impression on me. I then put it in the back of my mind. The very back as I began my career as a teacher and a coach, I did things in a way that was more familiar to the way I was taught and coached. As a student, I did not have a great deal of motivation to "over-achieve". I had, what I considered, just enough of a desire to succeed. I did what it took to pass. Having "B's" with a smattering of "A's" was good enough. It wasn't until later in life that I realized I could have, and should have, done better. I did end up with a 3.3 grade average in high school (graduated 133rd in a class of nearly 500). As an athlete, I learned to work hard because I did not want to be "yelled" at. Virtually all the coaches I grew up with motivated their players by raising their voices and spouting off negative comments to get the players to work hard and achieve the desired results. Nobody wanted to be the recipient of such rantings, so we all worked hard. I assume the coaches were happy, and I played on teams that were successful throughout the years.

I expected the students I coached and taught to have the same, or at least similar, ideas about education and sports that I had growing up. I found out otherwise. I could teach the motivated students (physics) and the regular ones (those who were taking the mandatory classes of biology and physical science). The physics class was a breeze to teach. They did a lot of learning on their own. I just guided them. The regular class I found to be challenging. I felt I was up to the challenge. Therefore, I tried to motivate them the way I was motivated. I yelled at them. I yelled again at them. I scolded them for being so hard to teach. My thought was, "How can one class be so easy to teach and another be so hard?" The required classes had motivated students in them and I was doing a great job with them. Why could I not reach those seemingly unmotivated, even after yelling at them?

As a coach, I yelled, with motivation in mind, thinking my players didn't want to be yelled at. Many had the same thought I had. They worked hard. Then some seemed to be deaf to my voice. They didn't seem to understand that I wanted them to perform a task the way I wanted it done. Again, more yelling. I became hoarse. Week after week, I lost my voice. It became a problem with me, but I didn't quit yelling. I couldn't sing in church on Sunday mornings anymore. To me, that was a problem. Something had to change.

Something did change when I finally heard a different perspective. It came during a staff development workshop when a speaker told a story of a man and his three kids who got on a New York subway late in the evening when few people were riding. The kids proceeded to run, jump, play, and otherwise, bother the other riders, while the dad sat in his seat with his head in his hands. The other subway riders visibly became upset when, finally, one of them went to the dad and insisted he do something about controlling his kids. The dad looked up and told that person that his wife just died, and he didn't know how to handle it, and that his kids didn't either. That turned the thoughts of the other patrons upside down. It also turned me on end. I came to the sudden realization that I had been trying to put my students into my box. Trying to teach them the way I best learned, on the field and in the classroom. How selfish! How ignorant! How arrogant! No one told me that I would have to meet the students where they were and take them where they needed to go. No one told me few would respond positively by just expecting them to want to learn a game changer. As I have learned, one who, when entering the game, changes the complexion of the game, or the direction of momentum, in favor of that team. The story of the man on the subway was the beginning of changing "the game" for me. I immediately changed my attitude and tactics in the classroom and on the field. With the change in my philosophies and teaching styles, came a change in the attitudes of my students and athletes. A larger portion of students were positively responding to me.

21

ALEXANDER

It wasn't until I became an administrator and assistant principal in the middle school setting, that all I had learned and put into place came alive. The biggest "game changer" for me was Alexander. He alone was the biggest reason for my approach to dealing with middle school students.

Alexander came to our school from Arkansas as his family, mom, and another sibling, moved into a house with a relative. That relative had a blended family, his three boys and her two girls. Therefore, in that house were seven kids, all middle school-aged, and three adults, two women, and a man. Alexander introduced me to special needs. He was an extremely happy-go-lucky kid, severely ADD (attention deficit disorder) and ED (emotionally disturbed). That was not a bad thing to me. What I did not realize was the fact that his medication was what helped him be "happy-go-lucky." When he ran out, it was a different ball game. He could not sit down. While not being able to sit down, he could not stand still. While not being able to stand still, he could not stay in a certain area, much less one spot. While he could not stay in one spot, he tended to roam.

As he roamed, he would open closed classroom doors, stick his head in, and just say, "Hi" to the class that was in session and look around as if this was the way things were done. The teachers would send him to the office. He got to know us, and we— him, very well. You develop a relationship with students you see often. Alexander and I got to know each other. Consequently, in his roaming, he would make his way to my office and stick his head in my door and say, "Hi". This got to be so bad that we had to call his mom to come and pick him up. We would tell Mom that he was a great kid, but he would not allow the class to go on normally and needed his medication to be refilled, pronto. Mom always understood and took him home, many times. All this was done with the promise of getting his medication problem taken care of.

One day, Alexander had started early in the day his roaming. Not being able to contain him, the principal, Dr. Thomas, and I would stand out in the hallway and keep him from going into other classrooms. He would head for a door and we would redirect him. He would head down the hall, and we would redirect him again. This went on for over an hour. Our counselor called his mom and had her come in again. We had met with her many times to try to find a way to handle him

And it seemed nothing worked. We hated to send him home, but school had to go on, and office matters could not get done. Mom was on her way. The incident was now nearly two hours in the making when Mom hit the door. She fired in with the immediate declaration, "Call DHS. I can't handle him anymore!" Upon hearing these words, Alexander flew into a rage I had not seen out of him to date. We heard what she said. He heard something quite different. He heard, "I don't love my son anymore, and I don't want to take care of him anymore!" He began crying uncontrollably. He nervously started moving around haphazardly then walked briskly towards the doors as if to escape, only to turn back towards the classrooms. The principal and I headed him "off at the pass" before he could get down the hallways and cause a commotion. Our counselor took his mom into the office and proceeded to call DHS. Eventually, we corralled Alexander into the principal's office so we could lessen the area of disturbance.

The principal and the counselor traded places in his office. While we were trying to calm Alexander down, the principal was going over some information with his mom. As I was in the office, Alexander lightly slapped me in the face. I understood that this was partly because he "liked" me, and partly out of frustration with life. I told him not to do that. He did it again, a little harder. This time I was a little more stern when I expressed that it shouldn't happen again. He intended to get me out of the doorway so he could get out and go down the hallway. That wasn't going to happen either. He smiled and hit a third time, hard. After warning him twice, and each slap got harder, I felt justified in grabbing his arm, putting it above his head, and putting him in a headlock where he could not swing his arm at me or the counselor. He began to cry again and struggled. I wouldn't let go. With each movement he made to try to get loose, I tightened my grip. He eventually quit struggling. I thought to myself, this might have been the closest thing to a hug he had ever received. I sure didn't do a very good job at it, though.

Representatives came to pick him up, and I never saw or heard about him again. The situation still haunts me. What could I have done differently? What more could I have done to make things better for Alexander? I couldn't care less about his mother. I never heard from her again either. Alexander deserves a better life than he was living at the time. It still hurts. I hope he is doing well, despite the incident.

I grew up in a stable home. My family consisted of "normal" people with "normal" relationships. My parents provided for my brothers and me and showed their love for us regularly. I woke up every day believing that it was going to be a good day. I may not have always looked forward to going to school, but I did look forward to living each day. This was my "normal". Alexander, and his situation, helped me realize

His "normal", as well as most of my other students' "normal", was not the same as my "normal". He was my game-changer. That situation helped form my dealings with my students from that point on. I would always have to take into consideration what each student dealt with outside of school daily and what they brought to school each day. I had "flashbacks" of the film I saw in college. I was afraid Alexander had become my "cipher in the snow."

"RAINMAN"

Many other students I have dealt with helped solidify my "game changer" philosophy, but most were a little lighter in nature. One of my favorites was a young man named Raymond (we affectionately called him "Rainman") and the impact he made on us on his first day.

A quiet day in the office is always a pleasant day for everyone. I was at the front desk chatting with my secretary when an older fellow, I would have guessed to be nearing 70 years of age, walked in with whom I thought was his grandson, a 6th grader. It turned out that it was his son, 25 years younger than his closest sibling. The boy had a "Dennis the Menace" type of haircut and glasses. He was extremely thin and had on a pair of jeans with a belt just below his chest and a cuff high on his ankle. He had large teeth which created a huge smile, and he displayed it proudly. The father was badly in need of a shave and a dentist. His pants were sagging, and his clothes fit loosely. His glasses were slid down to the edge of his nose, as he had to tilt his head back to see through them, and was wearing a "John Deere" cap on the back of his head. I greeted them with the usual "Howdy! What can we do for you?" The father introduced both of them and proceeded to let us know that they were there because the school they had been going to did not allow out-of-district transfers due to budget cuts. Since they lived in our district, we were obligated to accept them. That was no problem, so I got the folder he handed me and began to look through it while my secretary began to get the enrollment paperwork together. I noticed he had a newspaper clipping of Raymond amid several trophies and ribbons while standing with a rooster on a podium. I asked if he was a member of the 4-H Club or another group that would support him in showing animals at the county fairs. He answered me while, at the same time, adjusting his glasses without touching them with his hands. He squinted and twisted his nose and lips to adjust his glasses while answering me in his squeaky and scratchy 6th-grade voice, "No, I just do it on my own." This, to me, is a great characteristic for all kids to have. They follow through with an interest and do the best they can. Some, like Raymond, seemed to be successful. I then asked if he raised anything other than chickens. He replied, "No, just chickens." His answer came at the most opportune time, when he added, "I have a real big cock!" At the very moment he made that exclamation, one of my most "straight-laced" teachers happened to enter the office. She heard what he said and stopped dead in her tracks. On top of that, Dad proclaimed in his low, gruff voice, "Yeah, it's real big. You oughta see it!" I saw her reaction. She was mortified. She began to slowly walk behind the front counter while making sure she did not turn her back on anyone. I could tell she could not believe the huge smile I had on my face when this little boy and this old man said what they said. I took my cue, held up the paper clipping, and gladly said, "I've even got a picture. You wanna see?" I have never seen someone move so fast to get away from me.

That was the first of many "stories" Raymond gave me. When he was eventually promoted out of 8th grade (four years later –not the usual three), I gave him a baseball cap from the University of South Carolina, the Gamecocks. The front simply read, "cocks". He wore it proudly and came back after high school graduation to let me know he still wore it. He never found out the shock he gave one of my teachers.

THE EDUCATIONAL "COOKIE"

Public education, as it stands now, is under quite a bit of scrutiny. It seems, so many things are going wrong in all aspects. The test scores aren't as high as people would like. What to do with the funding is a big question, especially with the poor performance of our students when compared to students around the world. The problem of bullying is often in the news. Teachers having improper relations with students is also prevalent for public education to change for the better. I believe a big change must occur at home. One of our big problems is the fact that not every home is the same. Not every kid is raised the same way. When I interview prospective teachers, I let them know of their prospective students and how diversified they are. We have one kid who is dropped off in a Mercedes-Benz, whose dad is a computer technician, and whose mom is a banker. Another is dropped off at school right behind them in a pick-up truck that has a muffler being held on by bailing wire. The dad works in a machine shop and the mom stays at home to take care of younger siblings. We have students who have a dad who works in the oil field and a mom who works at a nursing home. We have students who live in combined-family homes. We have kids who are being raised by their grandparents because one or both of the parents live incarcerated in the prison 10 miles away. We have kids from all walks of life and family situations. They sit in the same classroom together. How could anyone think they have the same motivation to get through school?

We have a food pantry at school to give a satchel of food to some students to take home every weekend so they will have something to last until they come back to school on Monday. One of our students brought his bag to be refilled. Upon opening it, our counselor found several live cockroaches crawling out of it. Quickly, the bag was taken outside to be cleansed, but the mental images of how they got there were already in place. The student was told to get his book bag and take it outside again. The following Monday, one of our teachers was reminded of the incident on Friday by noticing a cockroach crawling up the sleeve of this same student. When we spoke to the young man about the prospect of getting his house sprayed for crawly critters, he said, "We got three tree frogs and a lizard in the house. Dad thinks they will take care of the problem." Tell me where this boy, and his siblings, thought processes would be daily.

I believe as much as the next guy in "raising the bar." There is nothing wrong with "raising the bar." We need to have goals in education. We need our kids to have a goal to reach something to strive for. We want the kids to aim at success in whatever they do. However, it seems those who are legislating laws on education are assuming all students are automatically going to rise to meet that bar, just because it is set. Not everyone is dealing with the same bar. I don't believe a vast majority of the kids have the self-motivation that lawmakers think they should have. Many students don't have the motivation we would like them to have. Sometimes I wonder what the goal of legislators is when dealing with laws or "reforms" in education. Do they want us to produce "test passers?"This may be a pride factor so we can say we have a good standing among the world's students. Or, do they want us to produce "producers," those who are productive members of society and provide for their families without too much strain? This, to me, is a more realistic and attainable desire. Many students are highly motivated and competitive. These kids seem to be driven for success and will work hard to obtain whatever their personal goals are. They will earnestly reach for a bar set higher and even challenge a bar to be set higher. Not **all** students choose that course of action, then you have those who are not so motivated. If someone sets the bar for them, they will sit and stare at it. They will ignore it. They will decide not to act upon it. They think, "What makes you think I want to go there?" I have taught students who wanted to be a mechanic or a welder. These are highly skilled vocations that take quite a bit of training. However, a sixth or seventh-grader sees no need to learn about history or how to diagram a sentence to perform these skills. You and I now know the importance of having a well-rounded knowledge of several subjects. I don't remember caring about that as a middle schooler. A good teacher will be able to lead them to the idea that they can translate all the information being taught in class can be, and is, used in the business world, or something that the student is likely to be interested in or even involved in.

I would like to see a lawmaker, before mandating educational regulations, make an appearance on "Are you smarter than a 5th grader?" I once watched that game show when a 5th generation "rocket scientist" missed the first question and had to be "saved" by one of the fifth graders. It had to be a bit embarrassing for the highly educated scientist to be bailed out by a kid 30 years younger. We seem to be better at things we are more interested in. I contend that if the question dealt with rocket science, he would have gotten it right. We do best and enjoy work more when learning or working with things, information, and people we like most. Students are no different, saying teachers work for only nine months is like saying accountants work only during tax season. Truthfully, summer "vacation" just means summer without students. During this time, a huge amount of teachers goes back to school working for a higher degree, attend workshops so they may get better at what they do, or even teach during that time. Others get or maintain part-time jobs to make financial ends meet.

I see, on television news programs, people getting to speak of the problems with the state of public education. They are referred to as "experts" in their field. After listening to them, I would consider them as "pseudo-experts". These "pseudo-experts" are those who have studied something from the "outside", not having been in a classroom full of students, not dealing with parents or family situations, and not having been "in the trenches". These "experts" use statistics to formulate ideas dealing with today's students. Statistics are good to have a point. They deal with a general population, not specifics. Students in the city have different ideologies than those in the rural regions. Students in the Midwest have ideologies different from those in the Northeast. The true "experts" are those who are involved in "it" and have been for a long time. They see the real attitudes and problems that arise daily, where they are in contact with the good, the bad, and the ugly of education. They devise solutions on a student-by-student basis, not a one-size-fits-all response. True experts recognize that you can't "keyhole" everyone. A "cookie cutter" approach to education only alienates those who don't necessarily wish to learn conventionally. If a student rebels against a norm they are expected to meet, rejection of the whole process occurs. These are the students who become time consumers in the office. When you try to force a square peg into a round hole, a chip or a bulge will develop.

Some students are bound for college with great motivation to be the "movers and shakers." Others don't care to go that route and are content with working in a shop or in the field. In my mind, these are the ones who essentially make the money for the "movers and shakers."

THE RIVER OF EDUCATION

When I entered education, I thought I would be the educator and everyone surrounding me, namely students, would be the recipients of education. Little did I know that I would be the benefactor of the learning process? It was because of this process that I learned more than I dreamed about the people I was trying to teach and forever transformed my professional, and even personal, life. Some of the following stories, and there are many more that are not written, are humorous and some are sad. Most of them are from my middle school days. They, as evidenced by the stories, point to an innocent, naïve, and even troubled age. I learned that the kids are genuine, impressionable, and vulnerable. I learned that even though the parents I dealt with mean well, the end result wasn't always what was desired.

These stories gave rise to what I consider "the river" of education. Elementary school represents a river above a waterfall. It moves steadily, sometimes swiftly, over and around obstacles. This represents both the excitement and boredom surrounding early education. High school is the river beneath the waterfall. It represents the maturing process and the settling of ideas and anticipation of the future of the student. It is somewhat turbulent and tumultuous in the beginning, but smoothing out the further it travels from the waterfall. Middle school is the actual waterfall. It is extremely active and full of change. From the time students come to the time they leave, it is a constant change in emotional, physical, social, and intellectual status. Middle school students are constantly jockeying for a change in their position in all these aspects. The struggles vary, but all are significant.

The following stories helped me understand what type of mentality I was dealing with as I first got into administration.

Over the last several years, dealing with students shed light on the way I needed to deal with situations and people.

I was introduced early to the innocence of the age when, as the assistant principal, a student brought a note to me that suggested I have a heart-to-heart talk with another student. It read, "He *looks like he's thinking nasty.*"

A student asked me during an open house if he could use the phone. When I asked him what for, he said he had to call his parents to pick him up. I let him know that the open house was for his parents. He's here every day! The parents used us as a babysitter that evening. *I felt so used.*

Upon receiving a referral for throwing paper clips on the bus, a student denied having done so. We showed him a video of the activity that occurred on the bus and everyone else that participated. We asked him to point at himself on the screen. He did. Shortly after he identified himself, the video showed him rising up and throwing paper clips. We just looked at him. After a pause, he said, "I don't care! I still didn't do it!" Later, after suspending him from the bus, his mom came up, very angry, to argue the point. "He told me he didn't do it and that means he didn't do it!", was what she loudly presented. We showed her the video and asked her to point out her son. She did. The scenario played out again, showing him chunking some paper clips. Her immediate response was, "That's not my son." *We don't wonder anymore where they get it.*

I was walking in the hallway away from the office during class and came upon a young lady who was going to the office. We greeted each other with a nod and a smile. I completed my task down the hall, started my way back to the office, and passed the girl heading back to her class. This time I stopped and said, "Say, haven't I already seen you a couple of times?" To which she responded as if she was a little scared at my question, with a quiver in her voice said, "Huh-uh. You've just seen me twice." *I wish they could all be that sweet.*

While in the hall during the passing period between classes, one student passed me giggling. Another student quickly came up to me and requested, "Would you expel him for farting!?" All I could say was, "Sounds like he's expelling himself."

A young lady was arguing with the science teacher about the sun being a star. The girl didn't think that was right. Her argument is, "Ifi it's a star, why does it come out in the daytime?" *Learning is a process.*

A lovelorn boy came to me and had a request. He wanted me to interview a girl he had a crush on and give him a one-page report on it the next day. *He will grow up to be somebody's boss someday.*

Another eye-opener early in my administrative career was when a 13-year-old girl came up to me and gleefully proclaimed the fact that she had been drug-free for 5 months. *Holy cow! Thirteen years old and already drug-free!*

A special education student was brought into my office for not participating in a class. While the teacher was telling me of the situation and lecturing the student at the same time, the student sat on the floor with his fingers in his ears. The teacher said, "I know you can hear me." The students responded, "Huh-uh. No I can't". *Fingers—the new hearing aid.*

We had a costume day around Halloween and wanted to recognize the efforts of a young lady in her participation and noticed she was dressed like a geisha girl. As we passed in the hallway going in opposite directions, I said, "Sayonara!" She turned with a hand on her hip and proclaimed, "I'm not Mexican!" *Back to geography class, she goes!*

A young lady from the high school had completed some work and had some extra time, so they sent her to the middle school to help a janitor. She came to the office and said, "I need a broom, can I have the key to the 'genital' closet?" *I hesitate to ask what she found.*

A student was in in-house detention for not doing work, and I asked him how he was doing. He said, "Great now. I'm figuring out the answers before I'm writing them down." *Eureka!*

While at a dance, a boy approached me and asked if the DJ made requests. I asked him if the song could be danced to. He said it was kind of a rock song. I questioned, "Yes, but can you dance to it?" He let me know you can dance to any song. I then asked if he could dance to "Amazing Grace". He said, "No! That's a patriotic song. You have to stand with your hand over your heart to sing it." *Therefore, there will be no dancing to religiously patriotic songs.*

A boy called the school to let us know he was sick and wouldn't be at school. The secretary let him know we would have to get him from his mom.

He said, "Mom thinks I'm faking it. She wouldn't call." *C'mon Mom, be a sport! All the other parents do it!*

A special ed boy with the mentality of a 6-year-old, not a 6th-grade mentality, came to me at lunch, crying, because another kid told him that he wasn't smart. I told him to go back to that kid and tell him he wasn't smart enough to know the difference. His tears dried up, and a smile came across his face and bounced right back to the table. *He may not have understood what was said, but at least he had a comeback.*

A student came to school one Monday morning proclaiming the fact that he had a date over the weekend. I asked, "Really? With whom?" He said, "Kristen." "Kristen, who?" "I don't know. We're only on a first-name basis". *It's a starting point.*

A young man was sent to me for flipping others with rubber bands, so I placed him in detention. He let me know he didn't care. I just looked at him. His flippant attitude continued and asked, "What would you do if I drove my go-cart to school?" I let him know that it was probably not street-legal and the police would stop him before he got there. "What if I made it here?" "I would call the police and have them ticket you." "Oh. I guess driving my go-cart is probably out then." *I hate being "one-upped. "* In a special education class, one of the girls became embarrassed at something that was said during class, and she covered her face and held her breath. A young man, slow of brain, yet quick of wit stated, "If you want to pass out, you can pull my finger. *" No comment here. He spoke the truth.*

We had a middle school dance and a young lady (socially awkward) was allowed to come to a dance for the first time without one of her siblings or parents staying and watching. She was in a world of her own and loved every minute of it. She danced to the music with ballet maneuvers, ice dancing, and the handrail on the steps to help her with some of her moves. The Monday following the dance she came to me, still excited about being at the dance, and gave me an idea for our next dance. She asked that it be dedicated to and have a "Celtic woman" theme. I politely asked her to take a poll of the other students and find four kids who knew of "Celtic Woman", then I may consider it. *I wonder why I never heard back from her.*

I watched a young man eat in the cafeteria for three years and after doing so, I knew his routine which was the same every day. I was so taken by the ritual that I asked other teachers on duty to watch as well. He purchased a chicken sandwich and chocolate milk every day. First, he would take the bottom bun and tear it (not bite it) with his teeth, twice, then, on the third bite, stuff it into his mouth. He then took the top bun, three tears, and stuff. The meat, he would tear four, sometimes five times, and then stuff the rest. He would chew everything, no less than four and no more than nine chews, then swallow like it hurt, and it probably did. He then would open his milk carton, partially, and pour the contents into his throat, tipping the carton 4 times, then squeeze and pump the carton. *To this day, I don't know if he knows what a chicken sandwich tastes like.*

A couple of boys were brought into my office for having a rather heated verbal argument that was feared to turn physical. I lectured them for a while and even though I had talked some sense into them. I went on and on to remind them of their friendship and not to let something so silly cause this type of action. Between points, I rested a little and gave a "meaningful" pause and stare to see if either of them would offer some kind of response with perfect timing. One of the boys asked, "What's for lunch?" I gasped, "Go back to class!"

Middle school boys are naïve and cocky for no seemingly good reason. Why? I still don't know. One day a boy was telling one of my coaches, Ben Roe, how strong he was and that he could take Coach Roe in a wrestling match. Coach Roe tried to play it off, but the kid was persistent to the point of making a pest out of himself. Having taken as much as he could handle, Coach Roe offered the kid a challenge. He told the kid that if he would make a fist and hold it in front of his face and keep Coach Roe from pulling it down for 10 seconds, he would concede and admit the kid was stronger. The boy took the challenge while the rest of the team was watching. He made a fist. Coach Roe pulled. The boy resisted with great effort. He grunted. He snorted. He got sweaty. Suddenly, as was planned, Coach Roe let go of the boy's fist. The fist promptly flew back towards his face and smacked him in the mouth. *Strong, yes. Smart, not so much.*

An autistic student walked up to me at lunch and said, "Mr. Nation, you have a bald spot (pointing to the back of his head) right here." *"Thank you for reminding me, Jacob. Go eat!"*

I was teaching a class on character and how to treat others right when I let the class know that I do not like the words "sucks" and "fricking". One of the kids in the class spoke up and said, "We can say those at home. We just can't say 'stupid' or 'retarded'. I responded, "Hit a little close to home?"

A young man was in the office, having been caught smoking a cigarette. As was the custom with having underage tobacco usage at the school, we called in the police to write a citation. He was asked by the policeman if he smoked often. The young man said, "No. Not often. I smoke a little marijuana now and then, but not tobacco." *Jaws picked off the floor. Kids say the darndest things.*

A seventh-grade girl came to show me a picture of her sister's dog that she had taken. She was proud that the hand in the picture was hers and that she was petting the dog as the picture was taken. She also volunteered that the dog didn't like boys. I asked why that was. "Because my sister's boyfriend shot it with a BB gun." I asked, "Why would anyone shoot a dog with a BB gun." She responded, "Oh, I don't know. He's Mexican."

I didn't have a comment.

Dealing with students is only a part of what I did as a teacher and administrator. I also had to have a lot of contact with my parents. I have been known to say, a time or two, "If all I had to do was take care of the kids, this would be a perfect job." Dealing with parents, however, helped me understand where the kids I dealt with were coming from. I have worked with some wonderful parents through the years, and their support and friendship has been priceless. The following incidents depict a different side of education:

While I was the assistant principal, one morning a father brought his daughter into the office and exclaimed that she was not to ride the bus or go home with anyone but him because she had been running away. The principal asked her why she didn't want to go home, and she shouted for all the office to hear, "I would if he would quit doing drugs!" We all

Just looked at him. He stormed out of the office. We took the young lady into the principal's office and talked with her about the situation and if she had thought to call the police or other authorities. She said, "No." "Why not?" "Because, I love him too much." Two days later, she and her stepmom came in with a restraining order against him. *While kids are learning, shouldn't parents be learning something also?*

A parent came to the office and told of the physical ills the family has been going through lately. They had been to the hospital. The parent had been suffering from "ammonia" and the young student had been suffering from an infection in his "upper registry system". *New diseases afflict students daily.*

A parent called in her son's absence because his eyes had been "double diluted". *I wonder if somebody might have been double-diluted.* At a recent open house, people were milling around, looking at displays and listening to the band play and the chorus sing. Refreshments were being served. A teacher at one of the displays asked a visiting student if they had a cookie. The student replied, "Yeah, but you should have seen all the cookies my mom stuck in her purse!" *They, evidently, hadn't eaten supper.*

A concerned parent was talking to me regarding a problem her son was having with another boy, "It takes two to tangle!"

One of our parents was having a difficult time understanding the grading system that one of our teachers utilized (weighted scale) and stated, in a phone conversation, "Well, I'm just going to have to come up there and you'll have

to explain it to me face to face. If you don't change the way you do it, I'm going to have to sue your ass!" *I wish I had a nickel for every time I heard that.*

Parents can phrase things that are familiar sayings and make them not so familiar:

"Really, what we have here is a catch-20/20 situation."

"I graduated as '**valedictorian**' in my class."

"I want to express my concern, but yet, not be accusatory."

"My daughter needs to be tested. I tell you, she has ADDH. She can't even cook and boil water at the same time!"

"How long is my kid getting '**expended**'?

I asked a father if he was attending his daughter's cheerleading meeting and responded, "Oh no! There's too much 'women-testosterone' in there!"

A grandmother, who was raising her grandchild, brought him to the office, checking him in after a morning doctor's appointment. She had made sure of the regulations for his new medication, an inhaler, "If he starts **whizzin'**, he needs to come up here and take his breather!"

An irate mother called me (with a problem of her son's doing) because my assistant principal (to her) was a bald-headed "S.O.B." her son was getting a referral for not doing any work, in or out of class. Her excuse was that there are no teachers up there "enthusiastic" him. "What he needs is something to make him '**antagonistic**'". She told us that when he turned work in, it wasn't accepted. She said the problem was, "When he turns something in, it's either **incomplete or it's not all done**!" *Instead of "enthusiastic" him, she was "nauseating" us, and they were both plenty antagonistic!*

A concerned mother contacted the school to report a threat against her son. Another student told him he would bring a gun to school and shoot him. The mom, understandably upset, said, "If my son gets shot, I'm not gonna be happy!" *That makes two of us.*

While dealing with a young lady with attendance and attitude problems, the parent posed to her daughter the ever-sensitive question, "When are *you* going to straighten up?!" The immediate response from her daughter came in an extremely sharp tone and left the room silent for a long time, "When are you going to straighten up?! You've been an alcoholic and on drugs since I was born!" *Now, are you beginning to understand what teachers are dealing with?*

While I was at the high school, a parent came to pick up a report card for their child. It had three "F's" and three "I's" (incomplete). The parent slapped the kid on the shoulder and cried out, "Why are these "I's" on here?!" *Right! Forget about those "F's".*

Sometimes you wonder where these kids are coming from and what kind of emotional baggage they are bringing to school each day. Sometimes you don't! Don't think that education stops with students and parents. It goes deeper. Other educators have provided a different look at what I have learned along the way. Yes, even teachers have provided me with material.

An anonymous letter from a teacher told me of all my faults as an administrator and the fact that all the other teachers felt this way. The very same week, I was notified that I had been selected as "the middle-level principal of the year" in Oklahoma. Talk about bringing me down to earth!

I had what I thought was a difficult day in the office. It was emotionally taxing, to say the least. A small group of boys complained at the fact that they should be able to have blue hair, wear earrings, or even dresses if they wanted to and that I was denying their constitutional rights for them to do so. They would take no explanation as good, and they kept on bringing it up in classes, so the teachers had difficulty teaching and the boys continued to be sent to the office all day long. It was extremely frustrating. I was glad to have ended that portion of my day. That night I was administrator in charge at a basketball tournament where I met up with a couple of principals from other schools. They both were complaining about their day and how it was miserable for them. I listened and waited my turn to complain. One told of his field trip in which a student shined a laser light in the speaker's eyes the whole presentation. On the way back to school, pop cans had been thrown out of the bus, hitting a passing highway patrol car. The other gentleman said, "I can go better than that." "How are you going to top that?" "I caught two kids having sex in the hallway at lunch!" After hearing them, I thought my day wasn't so bad after all.

Between lunch one day, I was in the hallway monitoring the student movement when I heard from the other end of the hall from a teacher, "Hey you Special Ed. Students, quit running!" *So much for confidentiality rules.*

We had to take a headcount of students during testing and one of the classes sent back, "9 **childern(sic),** 2 teachers".

During a meeting with a student who had been disciplined for spitting on another student, a parent complained that her son said he did not do it, and therefore, should not be punished. I sent it to the teacher who turned him in and when asked about it, the teacher said, "I saw him do it with my own eyes!" *So much for an advanced education.*

During a teacher meeting after school, while taking a glance outside, my attention was captured by a bit of activity in the parking lot. Two boys, who happened to be sons of one of our teachers, were fighting. Calmly, I asked if her boys normally get along with each other. Her response was that of, "Oh, yes. They are wonderful boys who rarely get upset at each other." I said, "well. They're upset at each other right now, because they are really 'dukin' it out." At this time, every teacher became like students and ran to the windows to get the best look, while the mom ran outside to stop them. *I think I lost their attention.*

I have three custodians in my building. Their work times were staggered throughout the workday during the school year but worked "together" in the summer. Early in the morning, one of them came into my office and complained about the work habits of another one, claiming he did twice as much work with half the amount of break time. He said, "If he keeps this up, I'm going to have to kick his ass!" I assured him I would tend to the matter. A short while later, the custodian that was complained about came into my office and let me know that the other custodian had been riding him hard and was getting his work done as best he could, and finished saying, "If he doesn't leave me alone, I'm going to have to kick his ass!" With a slight grin, I let him know I would tend to the matter. Shortly after lunch, the final custodian, a female, came to complain about the other janitors, stating that they had been fussing with each other and neither was getting their work done. She finished by saying, "If they don't shut up and get their work done, I'm going to have to kick both their asses!" Tempted to let things go and see what would happen, better judgment got a hold of me and I helped resolve their problems.

I dressed in a light blue denim dress shirt and khaki pants one day for school, and if I do say so myself, looked pretty darn sharp. I was standing in the cafeteria on lunch duty just chatting with another teacher when we noticed that a couple of kids at a nearby table would look at us and giggle. It happens a lot, so we blew it off. Another teacher was passing through the cafeteria and stopped to ask a question. With the three of us standing there, the kids at the table turned their giggles into laughter. We inquired about why they were laughing. They declined to answer. A fourth teacher walked up and stood by us as we waited for the lunch to be finished when the kids fell out of their chairs laughing. They still did not explain, but I did, finally, notice that all four teachers standing at the front of the cafeteria were wearing the same clothing, light blue denim dress shirt and khaki pants!

A parent, who was older than most parents of middle school-age kids, had come into the office and looked into my secretary for allowing his son to call home and ask for a ride. The kid lived 4 blocks away from the school and refused to walk home, so he continually called his dad to come and pick him up. I guess his dad had just had enough. The first problem I saw was the fact that the dad may have been upset at the request, but he still came and picked his son up.

An agreement was made to not let the boy use the school phone to call home anymore. Things seemed to be fine until a wrestling tournament was held in my building. It was chaotic at times, with students from my school going to class, students from other schools walking about trying to find the gymnasium, and unbelievable traffic throughout the day. The end of school came, which brought in even more traffic. As my assistant and I were directing traffic, this same dad pulled up rather irritated and told me that he was "pissed", and through his open window proceeded to verbally blast me in the middle of the parking lot. With traffic building up behind him, I finally got it out of him why he was "pissed". His son wanted to call him for a ride, but the office people wouldn't let him call, as per Dad's request a couple of weeks before that, so his son went to the payphone and called "collect!" The man had to have told me he was "pissed" at least a dozen times during the course of that conversation. He got even more irate when I asked why he accepted the call.

Traffic was continuing to build when he went too far with his commentary, and then I told him, "Now, I'm pissed!" His response, "How pissed are ya'?" "Pretty pissed!" As he slightly opened his door and banged it against my leg, "Are you pissed enough to take on a brown belt in karate!?" *I'm not sure why he didn't add a degree and give himself a black belt. It sounds more impressive than brown.* Trying not to laugh, I said, in as gruff and stern of a voice that I could muster, "get back in the car and think about what you just said, old man!" He slammed the door and took off quickly. Not to be heard from for a long time. That was not one of my most proud moments, but it still makes for a good story.

We had a teacher confiscate what the kids called a "shocker pen" from a student during her class, and put it in her desk drawer to be returned later. It was not and was forgotten. Sometime after that, there was a substitute in the room. When a student came to her to get a note signed, she looked for a pen in the desk drawer. The students described quite a reaction when she picked the wrong pen to sign with.

AN EDUCATION IN CHARACTER: COACHING

When I graduated from college and began to teach, my main escape was that of coaching. Coaching, in my opinion, is one of the most rewarding jobs in education. A coach helps build character, a sense of accomplishment, discipline, and comradery. A special bond is formed between a coach and the players because, during that time, the relationship goes through a series of ups and downs, through situations involving blood, sweat, and tears. It is a great privilege to be able to touch the lives of young men and women in that manner. To have contact over many years with so many personalities brings many tales that are re-lived at every reunion and even in between.

The many years of coaching allowed me to have contact with many characters. Every person I had contact with gave me a new perspective on life and how it deals with people other than me. Life does not deal with everyone the way it deals with me. Athletics helps reveal how others deal with life.

The chance to coach football came in my second year of teaching and expanded my realm of teaching, as well as learning from students. While coaching linemen through a blocking drill one sweltering afternoon, I was getting upset at the lack of effort being given by most of the boys. We had not had any success in the first couple of games we played. They were practicing like it and, frankly, I was coaching like it. I had to change things up and "light a fire" under them. We were using tackling dummies, and the boys holding the dummies were allowing the boys performing the task to do so without much effort. I blasted them for not working hard and gave them all I had about not achieving what they wanted to achieve without work.

My "wisdom" was spilling over when I let them know if they did not actively prepare to win, they were passively preparing to lose. I finished by exclaiming,

"Make him work! Give him some resistance!" I verbally blasted them. At the whistle, the next group fired off, and the fiery speech seemed to do some good. The boys holding the dummies began working as hard to hold them steady as the boys performing the blocking task. There was huffing and puffing and growling along with chants of encouragement from the players waiting in line. All but one group pushed their dummy the required

distance except for one. This lineman was pumping his feet, growling, and truly giving his greatest effort, but going nowhere. The boy holding the dummy was not budging, he truly was making him work. Everyone stopped and stared for several moments, and as the lineman finally quit, breathless and panting, and hands on his knees, yelled at the boy holding the dummy, "Gimme some resistance, will ya!" I looked at him. The boys looked at me. All I could say was, "OK, next."

A couple of years later, following a conference championship, I began my second year of being head coach of the 9th grade. We were to start the season playing in Hominy, a town 10 miles to the north of Cleveland, across the Arkansas River, and great rivalries. Our high school football teams have played in one of the longest uninterrupted series in America, dating back to the early 1920s. (They call us "river rats.") This year was the first time in many years if not ever that our junior high teams had gotten together to play. The anticipation was great. The atmosphere that night was electric. I was pumped. My team was ready.

It was late in the game. We were ahead 16-6 and Hominy was trying to make a comeback. They had worked their way past mid-field when their quarterback, Scott Harmon, (who ended up his career playing strong safety at Oklahoma State University) rolled out and threw a pass that was immediately picked off by linebacker Berkely Love. The crowd roared as he began to run it back when, out of the blue, Harmon made one of the most violent tackles I had ever seen. I have since described it simply as "He slobber-knocked him!" Harmon rolled around on the ground struggling to get up, while Berkeley popped up as if he hit springs on the turf and ran back to the huddle as we transitioned to offense. I watched the quarterback limp and stumble back to his, now defensive huddle. I called timeout to settle the boys down and make sure we did not make a silly mistake and turn the ball right back over to them. As I reached our huddle, one of my running backs, Ben Roe, put his hand on my shoulder and just pointed to Berkely. I said, "What's up, Berkely?" While he was uncontrollably sobbing, he said, "Coach, he hit me hard, real hard!" I put my hand on his shoulder and said, "Yeah, we know." We won. It was very memorable.

The first game of the next season proved to be just as exciting. We traveled to Hominy this year amidst rumors that they had a "move-in" from Kansas City. The game, in and of itself, was as full of action and thrilling as the previous year.

Late in the game, we were trailing and trying to make a comeback. Hominy was trying to run out the clock and we caused a fumble. We picked it up and returned it for what should have been a game-tying touchdown only to have it brought back because of a penalty. Player from Kansas City (Hominy) 24, Cleveland 18. We understand the boy from Kansas City moved back to Kansas City the week following Hominy's big victory.

The story did not end with the game. We loaded up the bus with about half the team. Many boys went home with their parents. I was driving, and my assistant was sitting in the seat behind me. About 3 miles away from home, we saw a flash and heard an extremely loud pop from the left side of our bus. The rest of the drive home was filled with discussion as to what it was. Our conclusion was a prank being played on us that involved some sort of fireworks that didn't go off at the desired moment. Due to the flapping of the stop sign on the bus that finally caused it to explode. We left it at that. It was the only explanation that seemed logical, that is until the Osage County Sheriff came to my classroom the next day and had some questions for me. He also took me to our bus barn to take a look at the bus. He showed me the structural damage and let me know we had been shot at with a shotgun on our way home. My knees buckled. Directly above the driver seat was evidence of a shotgun blast. Three feet lower, and I would have been in a world of hurt or, worse yet, the team, a statistic of sports-related violence. To this day, I don't think they ever found out who did it.

The reason I came to Cleveland was to coach baseball. If I was going to coach, certainly, I would soon coach my teams to a state championship. The season before I came, the team was runner-up in the state tournament with a few key players

Returning. I was excited to be a part of the team.

Little did I realize at the time that I had to pay my dues as the assistant coach. Part of my duties was to drive the bus home after the Away Games, a bus that was full of mainly Jr. Varsity players and no head coach, who drove his vehicle and then home, not necessarily straight home, after the games.

After a game in Tulsa I took the team to, what had become a normal thing, and that was a trip to McDonald's. It was cheap for them and free for me. What better deal for everyone? While I was making sure all players had their food, and I secured mine, I walked out to the bus to find one of my players in an argument with a driver in the drive-thru lane. This particular player was not known to be a quiet individual.

For that matter, he was rather abrasive and in constant conflict. This part was not unexpected. The fact that it would happen in this venue with a fellow who looked like he could be a combination of the lead singer in a 1980s hairband. And a part of the World Wrestling Federation is what I was taken back for.

I stepped in between them and had my player head back to the bus. I looked up at the bus and saw everyone on it with their heads hanging out the windows watching everything going on. They began to cheer for me and my players. That riled the muscled-up guy with great, long, curly hair, and he began to verbally spew things at my player again, which caused him to turn around and return the verbal sparring. Again, I stepped in between them and sent my boy back to the bus. At that time, I stuck my finger in the driver's chest and scolded him for continuing his "fight" with an immature high schooler and also added, "You better get back in your car, if you know what's good for you!" I have no idea why I would say such a careless thing, after all, I have a family back home that needs me. Much to my relief, and surprise, he got back in his car and peeled away from the drive-thru. The boys let out a cheer and I took a big, deep breath. That episode was over, I thought. We worked our way through traffic to the highway that would take us 40 miles away to our home.

The boys, all of a sudden, started getting restless, and even loud. I found out that it was the fellow who was at McDonald's who went to get a carload of his friends and took up a chase with us. They caught up to us and drove down one side of the bus, giving us the "one-fingered wave of disapproval". They then slowed down to come up to the other side of the bus to do the same thing so as not to miss anyone on the bus as a self-appointed farewell to the Tulsa committee. I wasn't happy with the actions of my players, as a few were returning the gestures. That is until another vehicle came up and joined the festivities. It was a motorcycle that was carrying a passenger who was wielding an ax handle. He was even taking swipes at and hitting the bus with it. The boys got a little scared when they showed up. They turned from "We showed them" to "What are you going to do about this, coach?"

I let them know what I at one time thought that the fellows in pursuit had no idea where Cleveland was, and that they would pull off once we turned onto Highway 412. They will peel off and think they had a big victory. It came time for us to merge onto the new highway. My initial thought was incorrect. They continued to follow us. The boys asked again, "What are you going to do?" I let them know that once we get through Sand Springs, they will peel off and think, once again, of their victory, chasing us out of town.

Once we broke out of the city and into the Lake Country, the boys let me know, "They're still following!" I must admit, I was beginning to get concerned. The boys told me to stop, and we would "rumble." They each chose bats, and they would give those guys the "whooping" of their lives. They were pretty bold as long as we were in the bus. "You can't hit a slow moving baseball. What makes you think you can hit a speeding bullet, should they have a gun?" Again, they became a little scared. As I drove further and further away from Tulsa I had to calculate what my move would be should they come all the way to Cleveland. Fortunately, about 10 miles out of town the posse gave up their endeavor of teaching "country bumpkins" a lesson in messing with city boys, no doubt, knowing they accomplished something big. My boys were just happy knowing when you're in a bus and being chased, you're pretty safe compared to when you're not in a bus.

I finally got my chance to be a head coach and, boy, did I have it coming to me. While hitting infield practice before a game, I was hitting a ball to the outfield and told my shortstop to move over. I was hitting right where he was standing. I proceeded to hit a smash which headed right where I moved him to. He turned around just in time for it to hit him square in the cheek just under the eye and shatter his facial bones. Not a happy time for me, much less for him.

I got my "payback" when before another game, hitting infield again, my first baseman missed my catcher by 10 feet with a throw and hit me in the face just below my cheek bone, next to my nose. Nothing was broken, but my face swelled like a water balloon. As the game went on, I had to visit the mound to speak with my pitcher. My speech became more and more slurred, and the swelling closed off half my mouth as if I had visited the dentist before the game. The more I spoke to the team, the worse my speech got. The worse my speech got, the more the boys laughed, though they tried desperately not to. That's not such a good thing during a game. I finally told my assistant, Ben Roe, who once was a player for me, now working with me, "next time I have to go out there, you're going!" The pain was lessened by winning the game.

Later that year, we took the team to Seminole to play in a tournament that featured a young man from Stroud by the name of Casey Bookout. He was destined for greatness in Stroud and went on to the University of Oklahoma to have an

outstanding career in baseball there. The tournament coincided with a track and field meet in another town. Bookout was involved in that as he threw the discus, he would come over after he threw and play in the baseball game as soon as he arrived. Fortunately, for us, he did not get there until late in the game. At that point, we were ahead 11-1 and had just three outs to go in order to "short game" Stroud. I put a relief pitcher in the game to close it out and preserve my starter for another day. He managed to get two outs by strikeout and still managed to walk the bases loaded. Frustration is part of the game. Casey Bookout came out of the dugout to pinch hit. The game just got more frustrating. Long ago, I made up my mind that I would never let teenage boys or girls determine my attitude about life by the things they did or said. What I decided at that time was tested constantly.

Kelby Edens was my catcher that day. He looked over at us to find out how we were handling the situation. Bookout's reputation preceded him. We signaled for a curve. It was in the dirt. Bookout swung. Strike one. Edens looks over again. Again we signal curve. Again, it was in the dirt. Again swing. Again, strike two. We had him throw a couple of fastballs that were out of the strike zone, trying to make him swing at another bad one, but he worked the count to 3-2, three balls, two strikes. Edens looks. Again, curveball, hopefully in the dirt. Edens signals to the pitcher. He shakes it off. Ben and I look at each other as if to say, "Are you kidding?" Again, signal for a curveball. Edens relays the message. Again, the pitcher says, "No." Three times we give curveball. Three times it was shaken off. "What's he thinking?!" "How far does he want Bookout to hit the ball?" We caved. Throw him the fastball. We'll see if we can find it later. Sure enough, the fastball came. It was belt high and left the ballpark in the jet stream. After all the players cleared the bases, I walked to the mound and asked what Ricky Lingier, the pitcher, was thinking. He said simply, "I didn't want to walk him." Ricky learned a lesson that day. If you walk him, you give up one run. If you throw him a belt high fastball, he will hit it, and it will never be found.

I, too, learned many things as a head coach and even longed for the time I just coached skills, not necessarily managing. My worst day as a coach came at a tournament in Skiatook. I truly wished that I could have that day back, on many levels. We were getting thrashed. The boys were not playing with any intensity, and they did not have an urgency to do any differently. The "straw that broke the camel's back" moment came when a lazy, looping fly ball went toward my right fielder who, while running in to make the catch, had to stop and slipped, causing him to miss the ball as it went all the way to the wall. The runner circled the bases for an inside the park home run. That made the score 22-2. Among other things, I was thinking, "of all the rotten luck." I looked around and asked the players on the bench if it was wet out in right field or if there was something that caused him to slip. One of the boys said, "he's wearing sandals." "What!?" "He forgot his cleats, so he's just wearing sandals." I came undone. I went to the pitcher's mound and began to wail. In my mind, I was trying to pump them up, motivating them to rise up out of their self-imposed baseball gutter and into a certain feeling of success. They would come away from this game, somehow, with a positive feeling. A lesson was learned that day, this time by me. It was, "if you don't want to be thought of as a jack-ass, don't act like one in front of a bunch of people." I haven't thrown a fit like that since.

My next endeavor came a number of years later, this time as a middle school softball coach. I told myself I would never again coach girls. I was wrong. When it comes to coaching, I'll do it, whatever the sport. I guess it's the challenge. Coaching girls is definitely a challenge. My assistant, once again, Ben Roe who has seen me at my best and my worst, took, what we considered, a pretty salty group of girls to Glenpool for what promised to be a great game.

After the top half of the inning where the Glenpool pitcher fanned three straight hitters, we went on defense, limping, so to speak. The Glenpool lead-off hitter promptly stroked a double to the wall and was followed by two more laser shots that went as another double and a triple. Those, followed by a couple of errors, found us down by a score of 10-0 before we could catch a breath. I went out to the mound to try to settle the girls down, with the intent of not making a fool of myself again. I was determined to use a little wit, much like that of one of my favorite people, Will Rogers, and the sports wisdom of Vince Lombardi. Truly, I was thinking of these things as I made my way to the pitching circle. Could I use this strategy on girls? Absolutely! When I reached the mound and all the girls huddled around, I made the mistake of asking, "Are you intimidated?" It wasn't so much that the question was a mistake. It was the answer I did not expect. My shortstop, after a short silence, spoke up, "Do you want to know the truth?" "Well, yes," I somewhat sarcastically responded. "Yes". I didn't know what to think when I heard that except, I wanted to make a point with an analogy that I was taught at a young age. It just didn't come out the same way. I proceeded, "girls, they put their bra on one boob at a time, just like you do!" Immediately, I realized what I had just said and was mortified by what had just popped out of my mouth. They cracked up. I was totally embarrassed, once again, this time for a totally different reason. "So play ball," I clapped my hands and headed back to the dugout. The girls loosened up and played much better. We had a great season after that. I was much quieter. By the way, when we played Glenpool at our place, we won, 1-0.

Right out of college, I was hired to be a science teacher and coach, head 9th grade boys and assistant high school boys basketball and assistant high school baseball. After football season was over and all athletes participating in basketball got on the court for the first formal practice. The drill we were running was a one-on-one drill. A particular match up featured one of the best basketball players in the state, a junior, and one of the best football players in the state, who had just signed to play for Oklahoma State University. The senior, who was considered our center— not an outside shooting threat, was dribbling the ball near mid-court. The junior, whose dad was the coach, was at the free throw line waiting for him to make a move. The coach, with a mouth full of chewing tobacco, hollered out for his son to guard him more closely. Again, he was insistent, "get on him!" At that time, his son turned and said, "he's not going to shoot from out there." The coach then became, what I thought, was enraged, went and grabbed his son and took him to the downstairs locker room where I heard yelling, banging, and screaming. Evidently, the look on my face was that of amazement and terror. The senior that was a part of the drill walked over to me, slapped me on the shoulder and said, "don't worry coach. It happens all the time!" The rest of the boys then carried on with practice the next few minutes by themselves, as if nothing had happened. That kicked off what would turn out to be a wonderful coaching career. That kind of incident really didn't happen all the time, but I was always ready.

Later that year, during a time-out in a game, the coach called the team over and was scolding them for shoddy play. We were ranked #1 in the state and the boys were not playing worthy of their ranking. The coach's son was usually at the center of the timeout huddles. Somehow, while his dad was scolding and getting red-faced excited, he made his way out of the huddle and found me, in my normal position, outside the huddle. He put his hand on my shoulder and calmly said, "You about ready to take over, coach?" I just looked at him with a clueless glance as he explained, "Looks like he's about to have a heart attack. Be ready to take over." I just had to shake my head. He was a great player with a great attitude and, in the heat of the game, maintained a sense of humor.

After three years of being an assistant coach in basketball for the boys and being asked on three separate occasions to take over the reins of our girls' basketball program, I consented to do so. It was not a wise choice. It was never my intent to advance in basketball but, after all, they did ask three times. No one applied for the job when it came open, and I was the "lucky" recipient of the job.

I wasn't sure how to coach girls. I just knew that I really didn't want to. My thought was, "Do I coach them like guys, or do I coach them like girls?" After years of reflecting, I concluded, "just coach them!" The problem is, I didn't come to that conclusion until after I finished coaching them. If I had figured that out earlier, I feel I would have done a better job and the girls I coached would have benefitted and enjoyed their high school playing years more.

Before the first game I coached, not truly having an idea about pre-game stuff with girls, I told them to go freshen up after the drills, before tip-off. My assistant and I would be at the locker in a few minutes. When we got there, we knocked and were given clearance to come in, we saw girls curling their hair and putting on make-up. I told my assistant, "We're sunk!"

TROUBLES IN EDUCATION

When I began my schooling as a kindergartner, teachers were scary but revered. We, society, seemed to think if it weren't for teachers, we wouldn't survive. A proper education was what was needed for a better life, not just a better job. I was in awe of my teachers. They intimidated me, simply by being a "teacher." I recognized their importance.

When I began teaching, some teachers were still revered, but most were, at least, respected. It was a profession that people held high on the honor list. It was just not paid like it. My first annual salary totaled all of $11,000 per year. I will be clear. I did not get into it for the money. I hope that is not the motivation to get into it today.

As time went on, the erosion of the thought of public education increased and public school teachers, as a whole, have become embattled. The extracurricular efforts of some or the lack of effort by others has caused society to put all teachers in the same category, even those who put forth an honest effort to educate their students.

I sense that the trouble we see in schools today may be because some teachers have lost sight of their purpose. There are many distractions, both personal and professional. Situations arise that divert attention. I believe much of these diversions are used as an excuse. Everyone has some sort of hardship or difficulty in life, but eventually they have to come back around to doing the job they have been expected to do.

We, as teachers, are dealing with somebody else's children, therefore the general public has a stake in what is going on at school. I've found the teachers that perform the best are those who have become stakeholders as well. Parents want to know the teacher cares for the well-being of their child and want to know that teachers want a better future for their child. If they don't get this sense, a lack of trust develops. The suspicion of "Are you really teaching my child?", or "What are you teaching my child?" develops. Sometimes teachers don't do anything to change these suspicions or stereotypes.

The media reports on many of the bad things that occur in public education. Negative press can be seen or heard about bullying occurring in school at a record setting pace. Sexual harassment has transcended the workplace and befallen education, and it is coming from teachers as much as it is students. We hear stories of "teachers gone wild", in that teachers are having sexual relations with students or are on a police blotter for drunk and disorderly or shoplifting. There is also an anti-union sentiment in many areas. Since teachers have the largest union, all teachers are put into that judgmental box. The lack of trust builds.

With all the negative emotions surrounding public education, people that are able, begin to seek out alternatives. It seems the current darling alternative to public education is the charter school. I contend the biggest difference between public schools and charter schools, even private schools, is the clientele. I contend that if you switch faculties, public to private, and private to public. You would have the same results. Any form of education that works for a kid is good, public, private, or charter. You find the winning combination and go with it. I have a suggestion. Since charter schools seem to be the savior of education, take the bottom 10% performing students in a public school and place them in a charter school. If it goes right, all students will benefit, both schools will benefit.

Another topic in public education is the safety factor in and around school. I cannot speak to anyone else's efforts on the matter, only where I am concerned. I can honestly say I would put myself in harm's way to protect one of "my kids." If there was a possibility of imminent danger, I and those who work with me, would do whatever it takes to keep our kids safe. I certainly hope a situation would not arise that would challenge my thought, but there are accounts of several teachers who gave up their lives to protect their students when a situation did come about. I would like to think I would do the same. I would like to inform the public that, by and large, that is the sentiment of the teachers your children are with daily.

In the spring of 2012 Cleveland was hosting an all school assembly involving "Rachel's Challenge." This is an organization that was being formed by Rachel Scott before she was fatally shot in the Columbine School Massacre. The premise was to begin a "chain reaction" of kindness. How ironic! Her friends and family decided to keep this lifestyle going and wanted to pass it on to school aged kids all over the country. The day before the assembly, one of my middle school students got word of a high schooler that said he was going to bring a gun and shoot people at the assembly. The frenzy began. The Cleveland administration followed up, found the suspected threat, called in the police and found that it was a rumor that had run amok and there was, basically, nothing to it. Thanks to social networking, people passed news of the threat along. Not knowing the truth and that the investigation had eventually gone to the early morning hours, social networking agitated a school population to the point that 40% of the students did not show up the day of the assembly.

It was a wonderful assembly, and it happened without incident. The school got blasted again, via social networking and the local media for even having school that day simply because of the threat. My thoughts came from a personal, not necessarily professional, standpoint. How could anyone think that we would allow kids to come to school in the face of imminent danger just for the fact of having school! They trust us with their kids every other day. Why not this day? We took every precaution. Over a dozen police officers were on hand and helped escort the students into and out of the assembly. Attendance was back to normal the following day. Not one police officer was present. Go figure.

The bottom line is this, any educated person can look back in their past and recognize a teacher that motivated them or taught them something specifically that urged them on to success or sparked an interest in something. The influence of a teacher along with what they learned at home is what places them where they are as adults. I am proud to be one. A teacher. An influence.

RELATIONSHIPS: EDUCATING EACH OTHER

As I stated earlier, I have been an observer since I can remember. Four years after I was middle school principal for most of these students, I was given the privilege of speaking to the senior class of 2006, the year my daughter would have graduated. My speech at the 21st of May 2006 baccalaureate service is the basis for this chapter. It was the 15th anniversary of the accident my daughter died:

"When a man's best friend is a dog, that dog has a problem."—Edward Paul Abbey.

"I have three favorite movies (those I will watch time and time again, willingly.) This is because I feel I can identify with each one. Some aspect of each of these movies reaches some part of my life. Some people may believe that my favorite movie is 'Batman', where the most prominent quote is, 'I am Batman!' Others may believe that it is 'Dirty Harry', where one hears, 'Do you feel lucky, well, do you?'"

While I liked both of these movies, I can't quite relate to them like I relate to "The Sandlot". To me, this movie is about relating to those close to you. This movie is about boys who loved baseball so much, they played it all the time. They formed a special bond while doing so. When they lost their only ball over the fence, they worked together to get it back so they could continue to play baseball. They had a common interest. It was their bond. There was unity and purpose in their lives at that time. The quote I remember most came from a dream one of the characters had. In it Babe Ruth spoke, *Heroes are remembered, legends never die!* While I know I will physically die someday, I wonder how long I will be remembered, and for what?

Another favorite is, "The Natural". This movie, to me, is about relating to those outside your closest friends. It is about a man who loved playing the game of baseball. He worked hard with his father to achieve his dream of playing professionally. Together, they made a special bat out of wood from a tree that had been struck by lightning. He finally made it to the big leagues, twenty years after a mysterious incident. He made the big leagues in a big way. He explained what his motivation for playing well was. He wanted to play so that everyone would say, "*There goes Roy Hobbs, the best that ever was.*"

My other favorite movie also has a baseball theme—"Field Of Dreams." I believe the message is about relating to your inner self. It is about a man who hears a voice telling him to build a baseball field in the middle of his Iowa Cornfield, "If you build it, he will come." The movie set him on a journey to satisfy his obsessed curiosity as to who "he" is. He continues to meet people who had unfulfilled baseball dreams. The story was a quest to "ease his pain." This was in reference to his own unfulfilled dreams. The big quote, "No *Ray, it was you!*"

The common thread in each of these movies was that of baseball and relationships. Your whole life is built around your relationships. The Book Of Matthew, in the Bible, states that relationships, ultimately, are broken into two categories. Jesus is asked what the greatest commandment is. He stated that we are to love the Lord our God with all our heart, soul, and mind. It is the greatest and foremost commandment. The second is like it. We are to love our neighbors as ourselves. The first, and foremost, relationship is you and God. The second most important relationship is you and others. Get your relationships right. Take care of them now.

You will always be identified, somehow, through your relationships. So, how will **you** be remembered? What will the people you go to school with have to say about you? What will you talk about when you have a reunion? Much of it will be, "Do you remember when…" Let me give you a thought to ponder. No reunion will be 100% attended. Some of you will decide not to attend. Some here tonight will not be "here" at your first reunion. Will you remember what I say tonight? Will you even remember me? I think so. You know why? **Bam!!!**

I am now officially a part of your brain. You may not remember what I said, but at least you will remember I slapped the podium and yelled **bam!**

Why am I here tonight speaking to you, slapping the podium? Unbeknownst to you, I have been observing you since you began school, some of you even before then. I have held a posthumous relationship with you on behalf of my daughter. You are a part of my brain. You are a part of my heart. Because my daughter was not given a chance to say, "do you remember when?"

I challenge you tonight to get your relationships right. Benjamin Franklin stated, "Be at war with your vices, at peace with your neighbors, and let every new year find you a better person." My daughter is not here tonight, looking forward to the graduation festivities because of one person. His relationship with a bottle of booze was more important than his relationship with his own family. His relationship with a bottle of booze was more important than his relationship with the people he met. Evidently, his relationship with a bottle of booze was more important than life itself.

I say, "Don't let your relationship with things be more important than your relationship with people. The people you are with right now. The people you live with and love on a daily basis. If you get your relationships right, beginning from the top, with God, then others, your inner self will be richer and your reunions will be sweeter.

Thank you for your time tonight. On behalf of Anna Elizabeth Nation, Congratulations class of 2006!"

ESSENTIALS OF AN EFFECTIVE EDUCATOR

A teacher is someone who has the ability to take information, which comes by or from someone else, and make it understandable to those who otherwise don't. Not everyone has this ability, not even some that are already in the profession. A teacher is a kind of "informational middle –man". Have you ever heard something and had no clue what was said? Your thought may be, "I have no idea what you just said." Then someone steps in with an explanation and your response is, "Ohhhhh!" A good teacher will help facilitate "Aha!" moments time and time again.

PASSION

There are four essentials I believe one must have in order to be a good and effective teacher. The first is **passion**. An effective teacher must have a passion for the subject being taught. It is not enough just to know about what you are teaching. Students, it doesn't matter what level, can sense a lack of interest and low understanding. If you are not very interested in the subject, you may impart information, but you will have a difficult time getting students to take interest in the subject themselves.

A video produced by Disney came across my desk entitled, "Heart And Soul." It depicted some of the what I would call, quirky people around the United States doing what they loved to do best. None of the activities depicted in the video really sparked enough interest in me to get involved myself, but what was evident in the video about these people was their passion for what they were doing. It didn't matter what anyone else thought. I have shown this to my faculty many times since then and expressed, "If you don't have a passion for what you are doing, get out now! There's still time."

An effective teacher must have a passion for the lives of their students. Teachers are blessed with the unique opportunity to play a major role in the lives of many young people throughout their career. Teachers have to seize the relatively small window of a kid's life and take advantage of it. The effect of that small window will last a lifetime.

As students see a passion for them as a person and a passion for the subject from the teacher, they will develop a motivation to succeed. There is a greater possibility for the student to develop a passion for the subject.

Passion will override circumstances. The thought, "I love children" in and of itself is not a valid reason to be a teacher. That can change in a moment's notice. Having a love for kids is a part of the equation, but if it were not for your passion, that love may not be restored. If a student develops a passion for the subject, or better yet, learning, the circumstances surrounding their lives can be overcome, which allows them to rise out of negative situations. The influence of a good teacher will go far beyond a classroom.

Educators need to remember this: No matter how unlovable students seem to us, their parents still love them. No matter how unlikeable parents are to us, their kids still love them. Passion bridges negative circumstances with each.

REASONING

If a teacher is to be effective as an educator, the power of **reasoning** must be displayed. When questions are asked about how to deal with certain situations or attitudes a student exhibits, the advisor could say, "Just use common sense." I contend that common sense is not so common. Common sense for you is not necessarily common sense for me. Common sense in one area of the country may be different in another part of the country.

Common sense comes from experiences. Mostly from the experiences of people who lived long ago. Things such as, "Do not run with a sucker in your mouth", or "If you play with fire you'll get burned." Someone had to experience the negatives from those situations and passed them down to let people know, it's not a good idea. A big problem nowadays is the fact that people ignore common sense advice and have to learn things on their own. Someone may tell them that is a stupid thing to do, but they do it anyway.

I coached a young man who was with a few friends, and they had heard something to the effect. If you soaked a towel in water, wrap it around your arm, and then douse it with lighter fluid, that you would not get burned. This young man tried it. I visited him later in the burn unit of a nearby hospital with third degree burns.

I remind you of that acquaintance of mine in college. He tried to jump from the third floor balcony, between the staircases, and to the first floor by hanging on to a garden hose he had tied to the railing. It snapped, and he fell to the bottom floor in a heap, split open his head, and was taken to the hospital. What I came away with in both situations was, "I don't have to experience something to know that I shouldn't do it". Somebody else experienced it for me. That is how people develop "common sense". It is not always exhibited in the Teaching World either. Common sense comes from knowing the people you deal with, students, parents, and fellow faculty members, on a daily basis.

I saw on the news, when sexual harassment was a hot topic, that a kinder-garten boy was suspended from school for kissing a girl on the cheek at recess. My first thought was, "c'mon!" If that was the end of the story, the only incident, and nothing else was involved, I believe "common sense" did not come into play.

I also recognize, as an administrator, that when you are dealing with people, you have to be flexible. I was on a phone conversation with an irate parent about a teacher's grading scale. The phone was on speaker so my assistant principal and secretary, who were both in my office, could validate our conversation. The parent couldn't understand why his kid got a "0" on a quiz and not an "f". I went round and round with him, letting him know essentially they were the same thing. The parent contended his son should get an "F" and not a "0". After trying to "make" him understand, I brought up the cliché, "we're talking apples and oranges." He fired back in a loud and harsh voice, "they're still fruit!!!" I couldn't argue that point. He then hung up. Know your clientele.

Another situation had a student in my office who had been there many times during the week already. Again, I had a teacher in the office along with the student, and the phone on speaker. The boy told me that I had better call his dad because his mom hated me and had some extremely vulgar things to say about me. The student actually liked me and understood his behavior was unacceptable. I called his dad and had the boy tell him what he had done. The dad began a vile, vulgar, curse-filled rant over the phone that covered every subject except the fact that he would take care of it with his boy at home. After I hung up and the student took his embarrassed face out of his hands, I said, "Phew! It's a good thing I didn't call your mom." Know your clientele.

As an administrator, I knew when I heard, "I know my kid isn't perfect, but…" I knew I was in for a longer conversation than I wanted to have. This usually comes when a decision was made about a student's discipline that was disagreed with by the parent. Information about things going on at school doesn't always get an accurate treatment by the time that information gets home. I have found that the truth is generally told with a slight twist that will favor the person

Telling the story. A parent, or even another faculty member, may disagree with some of our decisions in the office, but that doesn't mean we are wrong.

Knee-jerk reactions and common sense do not collaborate very well, in any part of society. Therefore, in some cases, we will take what information we have at the time and discipline a student, or students, and adjust as certain other information comes in. Once we do finalize our decision, it is because we have information from both sides, and have come up with a discipline that we hope is effective and believe is fair and consistent. "Knee-jerks" don't work when you are in public education, or any other profession for that matter. We have to look at all sides before making a judgment. No one can truly afford big decisions based on one set or side of information. I would venture to say, and have witnessed many times, that if the same thing happened to another student, and not your child, you would agree with us or even call for greater punishment. So, I will say that since your "common sense" and my "common sense" may or may not be the same, we will use mine in a school setting. As I heard while learning as an assistant principal, in a room with an argumentative parent, the principal said, "well, it's obvious we are on two different planets with our opinions. Mine being earth, we will do it my way." Lesson learned.

COMMITTED

To be an effective teacher, one must be **committed**. Teaching is a profession, not a job. As a coach, I wanted my players to commit to the task at hand. I wanted them to give me their time, their effort, their desire, their loyalty. I wanted them to be committed to the sport, and I spoke of that commitment often. As a classroom teacher, I wanted my students to give me their undivided attention, their effort in and away from class. I wanted them to be committed to the subject, and I spoke to them about that quite often. How could I convince my teams, and how could I convince my students to be committed to something that they did not see in me? Students are smarter than we give them credit for sometimes, and they can see through a façade.

One of the problems a teacher runs into is the fact that not everyone we deal with, namely, parents and students, will show the commitment we expect, or hope for. People will be "committed to", consumed by, "eaten up with", or "addicted to" things they hold in priority.

I have seen this first hand in the softball tournaments I have taken my daughter to. I have observed it in the world of entertainment, video games, and social networking, where people find it a priority to be involved in things such as these. That's where people invest their time, money, effort, and focus. Believe me, they have all the latest gadgets and equipment as well. Education, unfortunately, more often than not, is far down the list. That may be one of the biggest reasons it is more difficult to teach in this day and age. Education has become less of a priority!

The first football game of the season, as I was coaching seventh grade for the first time, brought a good example of commitment, or lack thereof. The team had finished the pregame warm-ups and had the big pre-game "rah-rah" huddle at the end zone, waiting for the results of the coin flip, before we headed to the sideline to start the game. We won the toss. We would receive. Being the first game of the season, everyone was excited, in the stands and on the sideline. We jumped up and down, hooting and hollering, and broke from the huddle in a dead sprint for the sideline. As the referees waited for the teams to line up for the kick-off, there was a delay. The referees were waiting for a couple of our "bigger" boys to come trotting across the field with pop and nachos in their hands. "What are you doing?!" "We went to the concession stand after the end zone. We didn't think we'd get to play right away." The other coaches and I were stunned. They had a skewed sense of commitment and focus.

It was difficult to find that a math teacher who was in my building at one time gave a large amount of math problems for the kids to complete as homework to be turned in the next day. This happened many times. Yet, every day he would leave the school carrying nothing home. Students noticed this and began doing the same. He expected commitment in his classroom but, he himself, was not exhibiting the behavior he desired from his students. As I heard in a good sermon illustration, a cow, a chicken, and a pig got together and came up with the idea to open a restaurant and serve breakfast. The cow would provide the milk. The chicken would provide the eggs. The pig would provide the bacon. The pig wasn't too keen on the idea because he would have to commit totally, while the others would just be contributing. In education, it's not just enough to contribute. To be an effective teacher, you have to go all in.

RELATIONSHIPS

To be an effective teacher, one must have a good **relationship** with anybody that is concerned with the job.

There is, however, the need for a "professional" distance to be kept with all entities. The news programs seem to be quick to report the errs of teachers, especially when the teacher errs with a student. With the 24-hour news capabilities that exist today, it seems these things happen all the time. Happening just once is too often.

The most obvious relationship is between a teacher and the student. I do not ever recall being told how to interact with anyone in the profession, much less, students. My very first day on the job I had outside duty, watching the buses roll in, assuming crowd control, and was just told to stand out there and make sure no one gets into a fight. Not too hard for me, but I didn't just want to stand. I went to the buses as they arrived and greeted the students as they got off the bus for their first day of school. I wondered why I got strange looks when I said things like, "Welcome to school.", "Watch your step.", and "Have a great day!" It was something the students weren't necessarily expecting and something that, I guess, had never been done. Especially coming from someone they had never seen before. That was just me. I'm not an extremely outgoing fellow, but I do intend to be a nice one, and I was going to express my "niceness". I did not set out to gain my student's respect. It happened, though. I was always out in the hallway as a teacher, and still, as a principal, want my teachers there. In the hallway, you have some kind of contact with just about every student. You are not shackled to just your classroom. Without a good and proper relationship with a student, a teacher may have difficulty getting work from a marginal student. I wish I had a quarter for all the times I heard the excuse of, "my teacher hates me", when a student is not doing well in class. There is no reason a kid should say those words. When a teacher has a decent relationship with a student, the student will be more likely to take ownership in their own actions. In a good relationship, the student will understand you don't pass a test because a teacher likes you.

A good relationship will be more likely to bring truth in a situation. A mother came to the office to complain about a punishment handed down to her child because when he came home he said he didn't do it, "my son is thirteen years old and has never lied to me!" I let her know she was rather lucky. My daughters had each lied to me before they could talk. When I asked if they had gum in their mouths as it wasn't supposed to be there, each shook their heads, "No." I let her know, "Consider yourself very lucky."

I knew he had lied to her before. Everyone that knew the boy knew he had lied to her before. She was just the last to find out. The boy had already told us the truth about the incident and when she finished her statement to my assistant and me, we looked at him and waited. He confessed. At that very moment, the mom said, "Up until now, my son has never lied to me." If we had not had a pretty good relationship with the boy, that conversation could have gone south in a hurry!

JT was another youngster who had been quite endearing through his time with us at the middle school. He would come up to my assistant, Mr. Cole and I in the hallway and let us know what he was thinking at the time, and even sometimes, let us know what we needed to be thinking. After a while, JT saw that we enjoyed his company, in short spurts anyway, and he, being a country boy, very country, started "feeling his oats" around us, and in the classroom. He was sent to us for acting out in class, which kids a bit shy of maturity do, and we had to deal with him. Mr. Cole told him that if he was sent up to the office again, we would take him to the woodshed and deal with him. We let him know, he didn't want to go there.

In the meantime, we arranged for the skeleton in the high school anatomy class to be taken to a wooden storage shed out behind our building and hung up. Sure enough, it wasn't long before JT was sent to the office, and we headed to the woodshed. He thought it was pretty funny at first. But, as we made our way closer to the shed, he started to get quieter and quieter. In his mind, he is mulling over the thought that, maybe, we weren't kidding. We got to the shed. I unlocked it and slowly opened the door as JT stood by Mr. Cole strategically in position to see the contents of the shed. I slowly opened the door, Mr. Cole had JT look, and he bounced back in fright as I quickly shut the door. I said, "That was the last kid we brought out here! I told them to clean it up!" We looked at JT he looked at us. Then we all broke into laughter. It was a fun moment. JT recognized it as jest, but he never got in trouble in class the rest of his stay in middle school. A good relationship with a student allowed that moment.

Good relationships with students also allow a boy named Roger to let us know that there is a dragon farm behind the school and also some alien eggs in the ceiling in several classrooms. Who would feel free enough to say that without a good relationship with a teacher?

Knowing and having a good relationship with your students will also help you know of their life outside of school. Situations such as a young man who hasn't had running water or electricity in his house in two weeks.

Situations such as a family who had moved to the area sight unseen to find out the trailer house they planned moving into did not have a roof, so they had to live in a tent until it was fixed. Situations such as the girls whose mom had died and their stepdad was abusing them. Without a good relationship with these students, instead of finding out the root of their problem, the reason they were not doing well in class, a teacher would just get upset at their lack of effort. Disinterest in the classroom.

I have wrestled with the thought for quite some time of why a parent would be upset with a teacher when their child is the one not performing well in the classroom. I have recently read in the news that a child made a "C" in chemistry, so the parent is suing the teacher to make them change the grade to an "A". Why in the world would a parent even think about making this request, much less, suing the teacher? I believe if the teacher is in contact with the parent throughout the course of the class, a relationship can be built and this situation would be less likely. I realize this is an extreme situation and not the norm, but it has happened more frequently than it needs to happen.

Communication is the key to a good relationship between a parent and a teacher. Invitations to visit or help in a classroom break down barriers. For some people, e-mail communication is good enough. Others would like a phone call. Face-to-face contact is the best. Both the teacher and the parent can put a face to the name or description and sometimes knock down a pre-judgmental thought about whom you may be dealing with.

Early in the administrative part of my career, I doled out a punishment to a student who had been what I now call "frequent flyer", one who seemed to be getting points by being sent to the office often. The mother was in the office when the "sentence" came down and all seemed to be fine. The following Monday morning came, and the father paid me a visit in my office. His exact words were, "If I had known where you lived this weekend, I would have kicked your ass!" I played it off and gave the standard response, "I'm sorry you feel that way." It stuck in my craw, big time. As time went on, I came up with a response that I swore I would have if this type of incident ever occurred again. My response would be, as I stand up, while walking out of the office, start unbuttoning my shirt, rolling up my sleeves, and saying, "Call the police and an ambulance. We're going to the wrestling room and will be back in a minute!" Fortunately, I haven't had to employ my decision. After time has passed, I realize the dad was just as frustrated at his boy as we were. He was just taking it out on me. If I had spoken with him other than just once, it may have been a totally different situation.

COMMUNITY INVOLVEMENT

An effective teacher also needs to be seen in the **community**. This would be especially true in the smaller communities, not so easy in a large town, but the principle remains the same. Students need to see their teachers in a situation other than that of a teacher. Students need to see their teachers as regular human beings. We have a life outside the school building. We run, jump, laugh, and play. Most teachers have interests or hobbies that their students find interesting. It is my belief that when a student sees a teacher as a "regular" person, they respond to the teacher more favorably. That is, if they see the teacher in a "good" situation. Granted, the teacher must not allow themselves to get in a position where students can view their mugshots on television. My high school counselor, Mr. butts, was, pardon the pun, the butt of our jokes. While getting ready for a special basketball game, my buddies and I went to the gym before school to practice. Low and behold, Mr. Butts was in there playing basketball. He allowed us to join in. Over the course of the next couple of weeks, we did the same thing. At the same time, we got to know Mr. Butts and started seeing him in a different light. We no longer made fun of him, but respected him and truly enjoyed his company. We saw him as a person rather than one in authority who lorded over us.

The media likes to report on the fascinating stories that occur with teacher/student relationships, which lately, seem to be sexually-related. There are far more good stories to be told. I, for one, found a great way to get to know the people in my community, as well as my students when I carried my skills as a baseball umpire to my new town. The kids saw me and the way I acted in good and difficult situations. I heard them tell their parents, in an excited to see me kind of manner, "That's Mr. Nation. He's my science teacher."

I connected with a different crowd when I got involved in community theater. My associations within the community grew a great deal when someone, while in church, which is another point of community involvement, found out I could sing and had a decent affinity toward acting. Being a science teacher and coach had a "strange" connection, but now, I didn't relate just to jocks, scholars, and the church community. I related to the performing arts community. I had now begun a career that included a partnering relationship with a whole town. People realized there was more to being a teacher than being full of information, rules, and regulations. Mr. Nation, they found out, is a "real" guy. A bit "quirky," but still, one of us!

EDUCATED BY "PEERS"

I have had what I would call a privilege to work with so many great teachers over the years and the opportunity to work with others. All have had some kind of influence on the way I taught as well as the way I handled myself around students in the classroom. I can judge anyone as to why they would have gotten into the profession to begin with. But I could tell from the outset of my career who was in it for the kids that they would be influencing and those who were not.

I began my career as a science teacher. Physics was one of the classes I taught. The teacher that taught it the year before was still in the building teaching another subject. I found out quickly, when I went to her for a little help to get started, why she no longer was the physics teacher. It wasn't long before she started coming to me for help in her classes. She whined. She moaned. I wondered why she, a teacher with several years experience, would come to a teacher fresh out of college for advice. I couldn't imagine what it would be like to be in her class. I wanted to tell her, "just don't talk."

At the high school I also worked with another science teacher who thought the best way to teach was to show videos, the latest technology at the time. True, there was quite a bit of good "stuff" on video, but not about everything he had to teach. He thought the kids enjoyed it more. I would go to his classroom to get something and would find the students lying on the floor, talking, while the video was playing. The kids complained about him a lot. This is where I learned that students, while they are at school, would like to learn something. They don't necessarily want their teacher to be their "buddy".

In the late 1980s the educational craze was courses "by satellite". A class, such as Russian, Chinese, and physics., would be beamed into the school via satellite with a little interaction from the students who sat in on them. The teacher who liked to show videos was the one chosen to operate the satellite classes. I think it was an attempt to get him out of the classroom. He was to set things up and then observe the satellite teacher at work. It seemed to go well, for a while. That is, until one day in a classroom across the hall from me, I noticed a slight commotion. The teacher in that classroom was a football coach. The kind of coach that gave other coaches a "bad rap" as far as teaching went. He was the stereotypical coach/teacher. This fellow would get the kids started on an assignment and sit at his desk doodling, what we think were football plays. This day he set the video in motion and, as usual, sat at his desk, doodling. The kids began to snicker. "Be quiet! Watch the video!" They continued snickering with a few comments spread around. Again, "Quiet!"

This happened again before he finally looked up to find some sort of foreign film, which involved nudity on the video screen. Evidently, he had the librarian tape, a program from satellite, that really did have something to do with the subject he was teaching. Somehow, the dish was moved, and it picked up the foreign film by mistake. The commotion came from the fact that the football coach, instead of turning off the television, tried to stand in front and block it from the view of the kids.

My theory is that the fellow who was in charge of the satellite classes came in to watch the foreign film, not knowing that there was taping going on. That's just what I think. It was never verified. I could go on a little bit more about some individual teachers that other students complained to me about, and I'm sure that I was complained about also. But the common thread about the "worst" teachers was that they did not challenge the students. It was assumed that the students didn't want to be at school, so the "bad" teachers did not want to offend them by trying to teach them something.

I have worked with far more "good" teachers than those I just wrote about. Every one of them did not mind challenging their students. None of the teachers were fazed by the whining that would occur from the students. I figured out that moaning and groaning occurs, even with the better students. Each of these teachers felt that they had a vested interest in each student. Something was at stake with each student they taught. The students felt this and they responded in kind. I learned early that if you showed interest in the student and in the subject, most of the students would perform the way they were expected to perform.

Until I became an administrator, I only heard things about other teachers. I did not get to see them "at work", actively teaching. When I was able to get into the classrooms, I found that the best teachers had control of their classrooms. The teachers that struggled in their classroom had seemingly less control. By control, I mean able to get the students' attention when it was desired and able to control classroom noise when there was a learning activity. These teachers were

Not always innovative in style but I could tell that the students were "plugged in". I have always had the "just teach" idea about the classroom. I have never been a gimmick kind of guy. Give me something to teach and I will teach it. I have greatly appreciated those who had the same thought.

I haven't named any teachers so far, but I will tell you about a teacher that made an impact on me. I know he had an impact on his students. Many of them told me so. His name is Marlin Ellis. Sitting and having a conversation with him was always informative, entertaining, and somewhat soothing. I learned countless things from him that I never knew, or at least didn't remember that I learned it, just by talking in a casual sense. He was an expert in the writings of Washington Irving and even influenced the placement of a monument in the Tulsa area from his input on the subject. I would go into his room for a time of evaluation and listen intently as if I was a part of the class preparing for a test. The kids would listen to him speak and, for the most part, respond as best they could. I know each of his students for the thirty plus years he spent in Cleveland learned in his class. I felt, even though he did not live in Cleveland or have his own kids come through Cleveland schools, that he taught his subject as if these were his kids. He took ownership in what and who he taught. At the time of this writing, he is retired. He was a class act while he was part of the Cleveland school system and, I felt, was the epitome of a great teacher.

I will give you an example of life as a teacher in a different light. One day while coming from the hallway into my office, one of my teachers was telling my secretary of her child and the discipline she was having a little trouble with. As other teachers on their planning time came into the office for one reason or another, a small group formed, listening and giving "expert" advice on child-rearing.

The teacher telling the story had taken some advice, of years before, to carry a wooden spoon in her purse in order to have an immediate consequence available. She had also named the spoon, "Mr. Woody". That caught the attention of the casual listener. We sat there listening to the situation, a little dumbfounded at times, when the teacher told us of when she threatened the punishment of the wooden spoon coming from her father. She said, "Do you want to go to school tomorrow and have to tell your friends that your daddy pulled out 'Mr. Woody' and spanked you with it last night?"

The group all looked at each other a little wide-eyed and I offered my own little advice to her, "I think I speak for everyone here. You need to change the name of your spoon!"

That incident was not necessarily an influencing situation, but an example of what we may see occasionally. Again, I could name teacher after teacher that influenced me positively, therefore, I believe students as well, but I know I couldn't do them justice or fear leaving someone out. The bottom line is that whether they were a "good" teacher or a "poor" teacher, they all influenced the kids they came in contact with. My hope is that I took what I learned from each of them and became a "good" teacher and administrator because I came in contact with thousands of kids. That's a lot of influence, good or bad.

NO FAMILY LEFT BEHIND

Of the many things I have learned by observing and participating over the years is the fact that family is huge in the minds of the students and parents I have dealt with. It is obvious parents want the best for their kids. I'm still not sure if many parents have a good idea what is best for their kids education-wise.

As I write this, I see a video taken on a school bus in upstate New York of some middle school kids bullying their bus monitor. It was despicable, to say the least. To me, just as despicable, was a heading on the news program I was watching, "the trouble with schools." That situation was not a problem with schools! It happened on the way to school, but how can that be equated with being a problem the school precipitated? That, to me, is a home problem. It started at home. It developed at home. Even though kids bring it to school, it can only end at home. Schools can put a "bandage" on the problem. Day in and day out, kids bring their "home" to school. We deal with it the best we can. Time and time again I see these problems brought to us, and we are expected to fix it. The source of the problem is not the school, but the fix has been laid at our doorstep. When it is not fixed, or at least not to the liking of those involved, somehow it has been deemed the fault of the school. How insane!

I believe the next big education legislation that is passed needs to be entitled, "no family left behind". The education of children begins long before a school gets them, therefore, needs to have guidelines a parent must abide by, and document that it was done, before a child can attend school. Before my daughters were allowed to enter a preschool program, they had to be "potty-trained". That was the main prerequisite to attending the school. The school was not expected to do this after they entered. Therefore, it had to be done before.

"No family left behind" should have some requirements for the parent (and child) before they enter a school situation. Should any lawmaker read this book, here are just a few suggestions:

- *Children should be taught to show respect*, and that in itself, will help them to receive respect. I'm not just talking about when they go to school, to respect their teachers. I'm talking about respecting their parents and other adults. Students so many times have the belief that they will not show respect to anyone unless they are first given respect. Respect must be taught that it is to be earned. I have witnessed kids who have spoken with their parents on the phone, and while the parent is in the office, with a great lack of respect. This is evidence of it not being taught properly at home. If kids don't have or show respect to their parents, and we see this often, it won't be exhibited to anyone.

- *Children should be taught that if they are told that a task needs to be performed, it should be done without having to be told over and over again.* When this happens at home a threat of consequences will be made by the parent and not followed through with. Have you heard something like, "if you don't stop, I'm gonna…..", or "if you do this one more I will…." If a child hears this over and over again with no consequences, lord help us by the time they reach school age. Students seem to be dumbfounded by teachers who don't give them a third and fourth chance at doing something. How many times should we tell them to do or not to do something?

- *Children should be taught that an education is important.* If it is important, it is important enough to be a participant in. It is important enough to be present at school. Employers believe what employees do is important. They require an employee to participate. They require good attendance. Schools do as well.

- *Spend "quality" time with your child and give them a good example to follow in life as far as actions in a crowd of people are concerned.* If you tell your child to "behave" and do not tell them what "behave" means, they will "behave" the way they think it means. Therefore, if you want them to "behave," you must first let them know and show them what "behave" means. The parent must teach them first, so later; they will know how to be taught. James d. Miles once stated, "You can easily judge the character of a man by how he treats those who can do nothing for him." Children watch as they grow up. Parents must be the proper example.

- *Teach your child to think for themselves.* If you don't, someone else will think for them. Have them work with puzzles as they grow. Have them work with their hands. Let them work with you as you work and explain to them things as they happen. I have seen students who have a high IQ (as noted on their standardized tests) who have no motivation in the classroom and get nothing accomplished as far as schooling is concerned. I also have seen students who are highly motivated to please and work very hard, but yet are not high in the IQ category. Consequently, I have seen the manipulative side of the high IQ underachiever dealing with the not so high IQ person who wants to please. The results are usually entertaining for the high IQ student and disastrous for the lower IQ person. Teaching your child what right is and what is wrong and when to do right and not wrong will be a great advantage when the child starts going to school.

- *Don't let your child quit something midstream.* Find a way to work any problem out. Help them to get organized and work on the "I can do it" attitude. If it doesn't work out, then, when it's time to sign up again, don't. Quit should be considered a "four-letter word" that a family should not use.

EDUCATING THE PUBLIC: MEETING OF THE MINDS

Any time there has been a change in educational requirements, it is always accompanied by massive amounts of paperwork. Teachers are no longer "allowed" just to teach. I propose that we let teachers "teach" and pay attention to these other observations that have been made over the years dealing with the idea that if public education is going to change for the better, it has got to begin with the family.

Parents, no doubt, say, and I truly believe, want their kids to have a better life and go on to college. Since many parents that I have dealt with over the years have never experienced higher education, or even finish high school themselves, they have no true idea of how to get their child there. Parents should let teachers and counselors guide them through the educational process. Teachers are in a position that seems to make everyone else think they can do it better than the teacher. Remember, teachers have been educated to do what we do. Let us teach. Many are being educated on a continuing basis. Parents do not go through training to be a parent before they become a parent. We parent based on the way we were raised. Even though you may know what is best for your child that does not always apply to the education part. We will not necessarily "dictate" your child's education, but let us lead in the process.

Parents should understand that, by and large, teachers truly care and advocate for their child, as a person, not just a student. Please do not accost a teacher verbally, or physically, on the phone or in person (or, for that matter, through the social networks). If there is a problem that has risen, let us know. We will be happy to work through it to the satisfaction of most. I dare say that there is more bullying going on in school from parents to teachers than there is from student to student.

Please provide your child essentials such as paper to write on and something to write with. The excuse of not having enough money to buy doesn't fly when we see and smell the effects of alcohol and tobacco in your presence. Priorities have a great influence on actions.

Peer pressure can be a good thing sometimes. Not too many times is it noted that good things happen when there are a lot of people encouraging a student to do something good.

Bullying is neither accepted nor endorsed. Don't think for a minute that we "allow" it. It happens. If we know about it, we deal with it harshly. This is where communication from teachers, administration, and students comes into play.

Help the teachers help the students to be realistic about the combination of athletics or other extracurricular activities (music and drama) and academics. The NCAA has it right with a commercial that lets people know that a vast majority of college athletes go to the workforce after their undergraduate studies, not necessarily a career in sports. Even then, a "long" career in sports may be over in the mid 30s. What then? Proper academics will facilitate a good job, therefore, a good life, afterwards.

I absolutely hate it when I hear the generic phrase, "The schools have failed"—or "The schools are failing." I have always taken it personally if one of my students gets mad at getting a failing grade in my class. I felt like **I** was the one who failed. **I** failed to do what it took to teach that student what they needed to know about the subject. **I** failed to reach that student to help them see the need to know what I was teaching. Over the years I came to the realization that when schools, teachers, and/or students fail, it is a team effort (or lack of effort). I also know that where it takes a team effort in failing, it will take a team effort in coming up with a solution.

I was in the office of my assistant Joe Cole one day when he was speaking to a young man about not getting his work done and turned in on time. Mr. Cole mentioned that he had spoken with the young man's mother and that she had tried and tried to get him to do his work, but to no avail. She promised she would keep pressing the issue. The young man spoke up, "My mom doesn't know what I do or where I am from the time I get home to the time I get up because she's always at the casino!" This was just one incident where the parent told us what they thought we wanted to hear. Maybe it was because they didn't want to deal with us or the situation in order to keep us from knowing the truth.

Teachers are expected to motivate students who do not have real support or encouragement from the home front. Parents, and I believe, the general public assume teachers should easily motivate their children to learn stuff in a way that the parent had no desire to do it when they were in school years before. The bottom line is, an effective teacher must, somehow, someway, excite the student to the subject. With or without support from home.

Principals are forever trying to come up with ways to motivate students to complete their work, much less satisfactorily. This year I showed a video that had gone viral about a young man in Ohio named Matt. He is a boy who is suffering from cerebral palsy and wanted to participate in the 400m race along with the rest of the kids. As the race went on, the video showed his struggles as his muscles tightened up. The rest of the kids passed him on the shortened track as he continued to labor toward the finish line. The video shows the other students continuing with their activities and the teacher, Mr. Blaine, walked to him, while he was running, to check on his progress and encourage him. As Matt "ran", Mr. Blaine walked with him, talking to him and supporting his effort. Other students slowly began to do the same. The longer Mr. Blaine walked with him, more and more kids began to join in with the chants, "Let's go, Matt. Let's go, Matt!" Finally, what looks like the entire class had cheered Matt to the finish line, to victory.

I saw two great things. One, the way the other kids rallied behind Matt's extreme effort and determination. Two, the way a teacher motivated a student to a personal victory. Mr. Blaine, without intentionally trying, motivated a whole class to do the same thing with a classmate. This goes back to the relationships teachers develop with students. This may not have gone down this way without a great teacher/student relationship, Matt may not have had his personal victory, and the other students may not have witnessed it.

I saw an interview with comedian Ron White that spoke of a Columbus, Georgia principal that had been "administratively reassigned" for playing a clip of White's "You Can't Fix Stupid!" comedy routine at a faculty meeting. I had a "You've got to be kidding!" moment. The premise of the interview was that Mr. White was going to Columbus to support the principal and see about his job being reinstated. The principal and I can relate to finding new and innovative ways to motivate teachers, and I was trying to do just that. His idea was, "You really can fix stupid. Go do it." Stupid is a knee-jerk reaction that puts someone in a corner. Now what? I hope Ron White was successful in his endeavor. I hope that the principal is still looking for unique ways to spur the teachers in performing the great task of motivating the unmotivated.

SO, WHAT HAVE I LEARNED?

Education starts early and runs a whole life long. To teach is to influence. To be influenced is to learn. The first teachers are parents, then immediate family, brothers, sisters, and grandparents. Then as one gets out into the world, we are talking about the influences of those surrounding us. Church, preschool, and family friends are more examples of influence. Then the world begins to expand, as a person gets older, and the influences become greater. A person will learn things from all surroundings, as long as a person pays attention to their surroundings.

What people learn as they grow up will determine what they do, where they go, and how they treat each other, as well as, life itself. It will also determine how they go inafter their desires, how they try to achieve their dreams, or even if they have dreams at all. One thing I learned is that the teachers or "influencers" in my life helped me fit into where I ended up. They helped me thrive at what I did, and helped me enjoy it all the way.

The following are another set of tidbits I learned along the way:

- Teachers work hard. Not in the physical labor sense like construction workers, but work hard in lives that are "under construction."

- Parents love their kids, despite their shortcomings.

- Kids love their parents, despite their shortcomings.

- Some kids, who seemingly don't have a chance in life, based on their living conditions and upbringing, rise out of their situation and become producers and providers.

- Some kids, who seemingly have everything and have been given tools to succeed, don't.

- Students are like horses. You can take them to the waters where learning occurs, but you can't make them take a drink of the knowledge that is there. That's got to be their idea. (guided by teachers, of course)

- Teacher's rewards are rarely immediate but may come years later.

- As for me, tell me what you want me to teach, then get out of the way. I'll teach it and do a good job at it. Period!

- I made the right decision 30+ years ago.

I wrote these things to convey to the masses both the plight and the pleasure of being a teacher. It is a profession that has long been revered, yet maligned. It is a job of which people say, "You couldn't pay me enough to be a teacher!" Yet, teachers are constantly being told how to do our jobs by those who have never spent an appreciable amount of time in a classroom. Thus, another Poor Richard quote, "Many have quarreled about religion, that have never practiced it."

A dedicated teacher must motivate the unmotivated, challenge the gifted, and work with an entire community of individuals to provide a complete education and give the students, and this world, a better opportunity to have a good life and be productive members of society. The sad thing is that not everybody has the desire to take advantage of the opportunity given to them. Thus, the struggle in education continues.